LAFAYETTE

88

RUGGED LAND | 401 WEST STREET · SECOND FLOOR · NEW YORK CITY · NY 10014 · USA

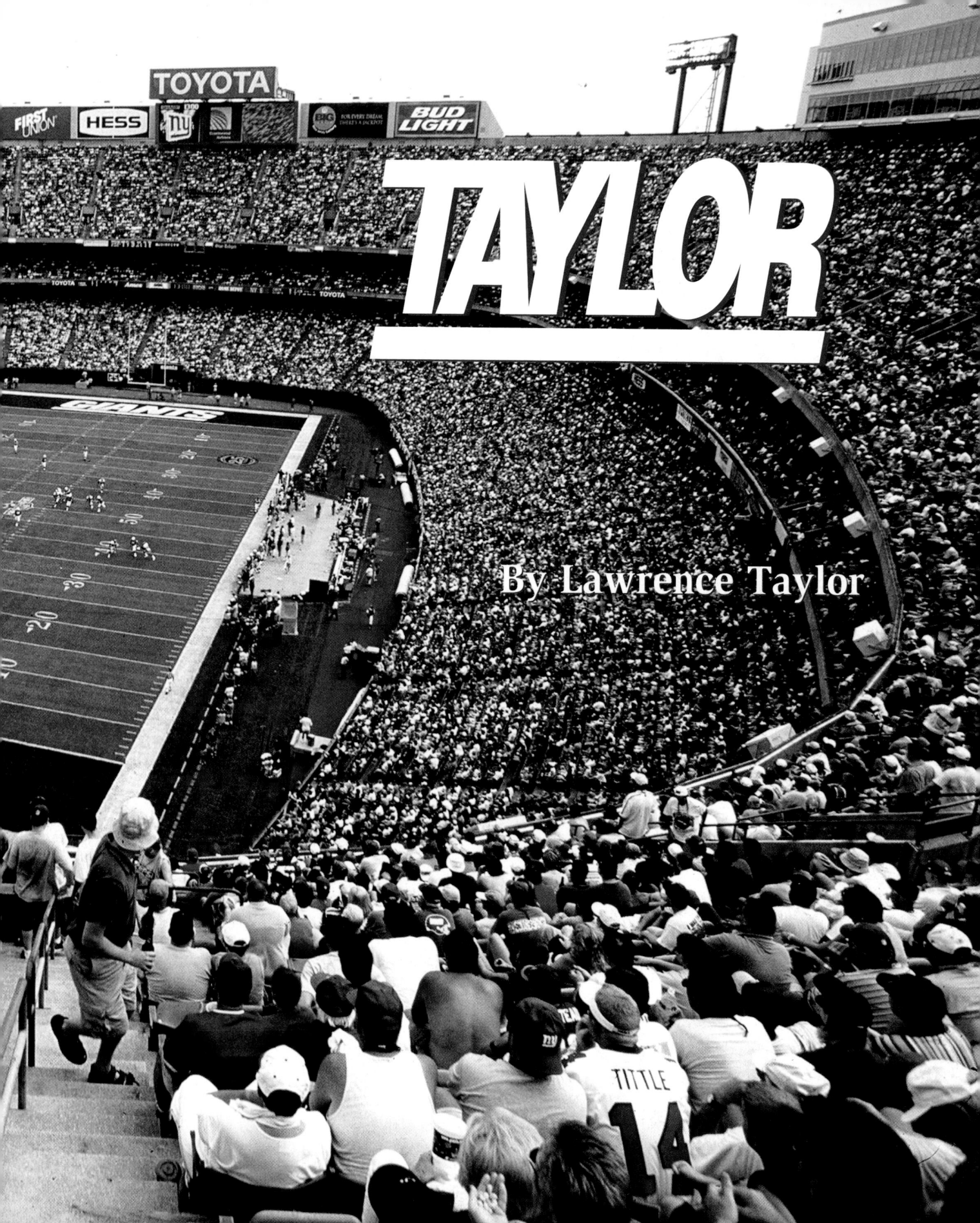

TAYLOR

By Lawrence Taylor

To all of the quarterbacks I had the pleasure of making miserable (Especially Ron Jaworski)

Also by Lawrence Taylor

LT: Over the Edge

by Lawrence Taylor and Steve Serby

LT: Living on the Edge

by Lawrence Taylor and David Falkner

RuggedLand

Published by Rugged Land, LLC

401 WEST STREET · SECOND FLOOR · NEW YORK · NY · 10014 · USA

RUGGED LAND and colophon are trademarks of Rugged Land, LLC

LIBRARY OF CONGRESS CATALOGING-IN-PUBLICATION DATA

Taylor, Lawrence, 1959-
Taylor / by Lawrence Taylor. -- 1st ed.

p. cm.

ISBN-13: 978-1-59071-082-1 (hardcover)
ISBN-10: 1-59071-082-7 (hardcover)

1. Taylor, Lawrence, 1959-
2. Football players--United States--Biography.
3. Linebackers (Football)--United States--Biography.
I. Title.

GV939.T34A3 2006
796.332092--dc22
[B]
2006016631

Book Design by
JK Naughton Design

RUGGED LAND WEBSITE ADDRESS: WWW.RUGGEDLAND.COM

OCTOBER 2006

1 2 3 4 5 6 7 8 9

First Edition

TAYLOR

November 18, 1985
RFK Stadium
Washington, DC

I've never seen the highlight film.

I don't need to. I see it over and over in my mind, and I hear it, too. *Pop pop*…and then the scream.

Monday Night Football. Next to the playoffs or the Super Bowl, it's as good as it gets. Lights, cameras and lots of action—America's watching.

The score's tied at RFK Stadium, 7-7, a minute into the second quarter. Capacity crowd and the house is rocking. Maroon and yellow everywhere. Fans wearing pig noses. The Giants are 7-3, a year away

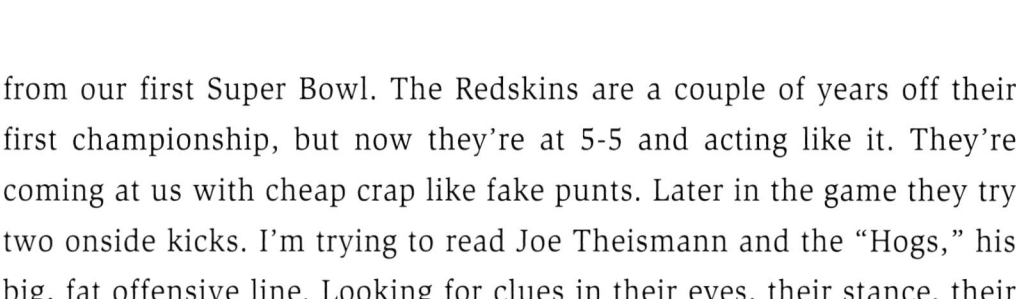

from our first Super Bowl. The Redskins are a couple of years off their first championship, but now they're at 5-5 and acting like it. They're coming at us with cheap crap like fake punts. Later in the game they try two onside kicks. I'm trying to read Joe Theismann and the "Hogs," his big, fat offensive line. Looking for clues in their eyes, their stance, their body language. Are they going to run? Pass? Something's up; I can smell it...but what?

The snap. The crunch of the Hogs against the Giants D-line. Theismann turns and gives to John Riggins, who takes a few steps up the middle—and whips around, chucking the ball back to Theismann. A flea-flicker? Come on. Don't come with that schoolyard stuff against the Giants D, son. Just gives us more time to get the quarterback.

By the time Theismann gets the ball back, his pocket is crumbling around him. Giants are pouring into the backfield. Harry Carson comes in from the left and Gary Reasons and Jim Burt through the middle. Over on the right, they put a tight end, Don Warren, on me. When are these people going to learn? I work outside Warren like he's a traffic pylon and leave him lying on his face. I cut to my left, curling around in back of Theismann. I jump.

Carson grabs a piece of Theismann's jersey, but the QB gets away from him, looking downfield. He steps up and is just squaring to pass when I drop on him, all 240 pounds of me. I grab his shoulder to take him down from my right to my left like I'm roping a calf. But he's got his right leg planted wrong. And as I pull him to the ground with me I hear that noise. That double *pop* that still makes me want to puke.

We're going down when Reasons and Burt jump on and add their 500 pounds to the pile. Riggins joins in with a little shoving, too.

Now there's another noise. A scream. "You broke my leg!"

Let me tell you, pileups are ugly places. Ugly things happen in there, and nobody cares about anybody else. The only law is survival. But you never saw guys flying off a pile so fast. I take a quick look down at Theismann.

You ever hear the term *compound fracture*? It means this: the bone is sticking right out of the leg. And that's what's going on with Joe. His leg's bent at an angle that is just *wrong*, and below that, there's some white hard stuff sticking out of his skin under his maroon pants.

I jump up like there's a fire and wave over to the Redskins trainer. Jim Burt is doing the same thing. We both put our hands over our helmets. We just cannot believe what we are seeing.

Pretty soon they've got Theismann on a cart. Joe's all there the whole time. He's not in shock. The man's a warrior, I got to give him that. As they're taking him away he yells out to Carson that he's going to come back and beat the Giants before Harry retires. Carson just shakes his head.

"Maybe, pal, but it ain't gonna be tonight."

Jay Schroeder came in and led the Redskins to a come-from-behind victory. Of course they were all playing for Theismann.

Personally, I ended up having a great game. I was shaken up at the time, yeah, but I finished with eleven tackles, two sacks and a fumble recovery.

And I didn't feel guilty about Theismann.

I didn't like breaking his leg, and I sure as hell hadn't tried to. But this is a violent sport. I was just doing my job. You take risks when you step out on the field against someone like me.

Years later, Joe asked me on TV what effect that moment had on me. I didn't have to think about it. No matter how great you are, I told him, it can be over in an instant.

Reason enough to live life at full speed.

I called Theismann in the hospital the next day. Some woman answered the phone, his girlfriend or wife. "Joe, Joe," she said. "It's that guy!"

I said hi. "How you doing there?"

"Not very well."

"Why?"

"You broke both bones in my leg."

"Joe," I said, "you gotta understand—I don't do things halfway."

CHAPTER 01 | Restless In Lightfoot

Jaycees, D'Fellas and Dad's Belt

I always did love contact.

Living off the two-lane highway in Lightfoot, Virginia, with nobody around but me and my brothers for most of the day, I used to race out to meet my dad when he came home from the shipyard just so I could put a good hit on him.

"When Lawrence was little," my dad says, "we just got out there and played together. He never liked to stop playing 'til he won. One thing was—he always liked to hit. He'd grab me around the legs and he wouldn't let go."

"I got you that time, Dad," I'd say to him.

"Well, when he was nine or ten, Lawrence was already tackling me. As he got to eleven, twelve, thirteen, I had to put a little muscle into it. I had to get a little rough with him. He liked contact."

I was one of three boys growing up in Lightfoot, a speck of a town on the edge of Williamsburg, Virginia. We were all high energy and a little out of control—but especially me. I was basically a good kid—I was polite, sweet, even—but I had an itch inside I could never seem to scratch.

I was always getting into something, and usually dragging my brothers Buddy and Kim into it, too. I was the one coming up with the schemes. We'd climb trees, like all kids, but I thought, come on, there's got to be something more to this, let's do it Tarzan-style, leap from one tree to another. The branch on the second tree didn't hold, and I fell about twenty feet to the ground and nearly broke my arm. As soon as I wiped off the blood, though, I was climbing up another tree to try it again. Avoiding pain never meant much to me—at least not as much as the buzz I got from visiting the wild side.

We lived in a simple, four-room frame house back in the woods a bit from the road. The closest neighbors were either clear across the road or back through the woods. Mom and Dad were always working. We had some babysitters in our early years—but mostly it was just me, Buddy and Kim. So I learned to act on my own, and to not wait around for anybody to tell me what to do.

There were some basic realities that kept me on the ground. First, chores—a lot of them. (A lot of my scheming was around how to get Buddy and Kim to do my share.) Then there was Mom's spy network. She had informers all over Williamsburg who would tell her who I was with and what I was doing, where and when. On top of that, there were curfews. And my folks were believers in old-school discipline, too.

Things were basically set up as much as possible to keep me from getting out in the world and into trouble. From having too much fun, in

"You could say I resisted instruction."

other words—especially as I got older. But that didn't keep me from trying. In fact, it made me be even sneakier and more creative.

My personality made me push the edges, see what I could get out of life. If it wasn't for my parents being so hard-nosed, I probably would have gotten out of Lightfoot and clear out of Virginia. Who knows where I would have ended up? It wouldn't have been the Pro Football Hall of Fame, though.

Being black in those days and not having had the chance to go to college, my folks had to do what they could to keep us fed. My mom, Iris, worked different low-paying jobs. My dad, Clarence, was a dispatcher at the Newport News shipyard. Like a lot of black families, we didn't have but the necessities, and sometimes barely that, but we always ate all right and I grew up big and strong enough to get called "Monster." When Mom and Dad were home they spent good time with us—Mom especially—and all in all we were a pretty close family.

Besides being my jailer, Mom was my inspiration and life coach. She put everything into raising her kids as best she could. Mom gave us all good, solid values and encouraged us to go to college so we could have the opportunities she never had. After working long days as a cashier or clerk she used to tutor and drill us in the evenings. With me it was sometimes like pulling teeth—I was bright enough, and I had a good memory, but you could say I resisted instruction. If I wasn't going to figure it out my way, I wasn't really interested. That was the story with school, too—I did what I had to to get by, but I didn't *apply* myself real often.

Probably the best way to get me to really go for it was to tell me I couldn't do it. I don't know if Mom ever figured that one out. (A few coaches and players learned it the hard way, though.)

On Friday evenings, Mom would get us all together just to talk about stuff that was on our minds. Mom made sure we went to church. She brought God into our lives—and even in my darkest days, he's been there since.

I picked up my toughness from both my parents. I have never known two people who've worked so hard and sacrificed so much to give their kids a good life. But Dad was probably where I got my physicality. If it was a sport, he could do it well: he was a boxer, a baseball player and he played a mean game of hoop. He used to try to get me to go running with him when I was with the Giants, just so he could kick my butt. Probably still could.

But he wasn't just a jock, he *knows* so much about sports. He'd watch football all day Sunday. My brothers were more into that than me—I've always been more a doer than a watcher. But sometimes I'd get talked into sticking around and Dad would analyze every play backwards and forwards, looking at it in a way I only started to when I played at the pro level. He tried to point out some of the stud players at that time, quarterbacks like Roger Staubach or Ken Stabler.

But I was more interested in the defense. I remember watching a Bears game with him. I forget who they were playing, but I do remember Dick Butkus just destroying everything in his path. I loved Butkus's attitude, his take-no-prisoners approach, the way he owned the damn field. My dad pointed out how Butkus used to strip the ball from backs and QBs. That must have made an impression, because the strip move is something I brought back to the game—playing *offensive* defense.

But like I said, instead of sitting on my butt watching TV, my thing was, let's go out and hammer on guys, play ball, have fun.

And that's what I did.

Me and a bunch of other guys played on weekends, on Thanksgiving, during lunch hour at school. Full tackle, no pads, thirty a side. Coming into class covered with dirt, stinking to high heaven—and loving it. But I didn't join a school team until I was a junior in high school. I didn't want that organized, regimented business. I saw our Lafayette High School team

practicing and didn't like the idea of all the drills, the memorizing of plays and the preachy stuff on how you were supposed to carry yourself. Seemed like a waste of time.

Plus, here I was, 5'7", maybe 5'8" and *man*—the dudes on the school team were huge!

But now I wouldn't be writing this book unless I did get into organized football somewhere along the line.

Thing is, I've never been a big planner.

My whole style, my whole life, is lived in the moment. *This* moment. Right now. I didn't have any notions of getting to the NFL or even playing college ball. So to get me there, God, fate, *something* had to reach out, grab me and pull me in. And the first thing that got me was just the chance to get out of Williamsburg. For one weekend road trip.

In those days, baseball was my main game. I was on the Lafayette team, and I was a damn good catcher. I could hit it a mile and could throw out runners at second from the squat. One day at the beginning of my sophomore year, Pete Babcock, the coach of the Williamsburg city rec league football team, was watching me at baseball practice and thought I'd probably make a good football player.

Nah, I thought. I liked where things were going with baseball, and who was this guy, anyway? But he was holding an ace up his sleeve. I found out the next day that his Jaycee team was going to be playing an away game against a Jaycee squad from Pittsburgh that year. Pittsburgh, PA! *Dag!* For a restless kid who'd never been out of Williamsburg, it might as well have been Paris—or Mars. And going with a bunch of other kids—and no parents?

Sign me up!

So I joined the Jaycees. I was gawky, like kids are at that age, and I sure didn't know about the fine points of the game, but I had a feel for it right away and I started to play pretty well for them. I had decided from the start that defense is where I wanted to be. I would rather hit than *be* hit. Coach Babcock made me out for a linebacker. And that was fine with me—linebackers were the ones controlling the action on the defense.

I began to get into this whole defensive mindset, too. I did some reading, checked out some of the linebacking greats—Sam Huff, Ray Nitschke, Butkus. I started to see that A, they were smart, had a vision of everything that was happening on the field. And B, for them, the game was about complete domination. They were *mean*. And there was something I really liked about that. I was always a pretty nice kid, like I said. Polite, *yes, please, no, thank you.* But I was also about the wildest thing you could stuff into a kid's body. So I was seeing, for the first time, where that wildness could go.

Still, though, it was all about getting to Pittsburgh. It turned out to be a big, hilly, gray city where people looked different, talked different, thought different. It stoked my appetite to see more of the world. We got whupped pretty bad in the game, by the way. Hard hitting, kids getting knocked out of the game, snow on the ground—nasty, AFC Central stuff. Fun, in other words.

And back in Williamsburg, fate threw something else out at me to drag me onto the high school team. Literally.

Coach Jones, the Lafayette running backs and linebackers coach, was on the prowl. He was always looking for players for the football team— he'd take one look at you just standing in the hall and know if you could play. Didn't know me from Adam, but figured I was built like a football player. On the small side, maybe, but then I was young. He knew I'd grow. So one day he came up and asked me, "Hey, man, are you playing football?"

I told him I was playing with the Jaycees. He practically laughed in my face. Told me they were the peewee leagues, that it was never going to get me into the papers, into college ball, anywhere at all. Did the hard sell. Now, you have to understand, Coach Jones is a force of nature. He was all God and football and motivation and little rhyming slogans, and he'd recruit his own mom if he thought she could help the team. So he talked me into joining the Lafayette Rams when I was a junior. I figured it was a step up from Jaycee ball, and maybe it would be a good time. But mainly I said yes just to get Coach off my back.

And he didn't miss a chance to remind me—especially when he saw me with some girl.

"You hear that, honey? He's coming out for the team next year—make sure he don't lie to me!"

Junior year rolled around and I signed up—and regretted it almost right away.

The drills. The hitting. The 200 pound linemen! Damn!

I was small, I had missed two years of high school ball and I was getting pushed around and beat up. I was a defensive end, a tackle, a guard, a center—and in each position I was getting my rear end handed to me on a platter. Finally, at one practice where I was taking one big hit after another, I decided I was not getting anywhere, and never would. I walked off the field.

"I'm outta here," I said. "I quit!"

Up came Coach Jones, all fire and brimstone. He followed me into the locker room and started up with the preaching, shouting, "You made a commitment, and it said nothing about walking away! You've got to *finish*, man! And you're going to stay here this year and do it, and I don't care if they beat your butt all over the field!" He went on like that for about ten minutes. I put up some kind of weak fight, but the result was I went back and finished the drills.

I might have stuck with it because the only thing tougher than getting beat on and exhausted was Coach Jones putting a fire under your backside.

No escape from it at home, either. Dad encouraged me to go out there and get my butt kicked so I could get up and do it again. Great.

So quitting was out. I suffered through the preseason and then the first half of the season. I was getting better as my body got used to the abuse and I started to really learn the game. But all I was doing in games was keeping the bench good and warm.

The season went on and I hadn't played once. About halfway through our schedule, we came up on our biggest game: Bethel High. Bethel was our biggest rival and one of the best teams in the league that year. The stands were packed for that game—Dad, Mom and 10,000 other people were screaming their heads off. It was cold and rainy and as usual, Bethel played us tough. With no score in a hard-hitting game in the mud, Bethel had the ball and was marching down the field. Tony McConnel, our defensive end—my position—was having a bad night. Bethel was sending runners around, over and right through him.

Finally our head coach, Mike Bucci, turned around and said, "Taylor! Get ready!"

Now? Aww, why *now* of all moments? I was shaking, my mouth was dry and I felt like I was about to puke. No time to think about it, though—the next thing I knew I was running around, chasing people, making tackles, driving Bethel players into the mud. *Whap!* I sacked their quarterback! *Zap*! I tipped a pass, intercepted it and ran it back down the sideline for a

touchdown! My adrenaline was going through the roof. I couldn't get enough of this.

The game was basically just defenses kicking the crap out of offenses. It was still scoreless in the last minute of the fourth quarter, when Bethel was forced to punt from their own end zone.

On the snap I lunged, leaped—and blocked the punt! We recovered for the winning touchdown.

In all my life until then, of chasing through the woods, jumping out of trees and hitting home runs, I had never had a feeling like that. I was revved up, out-of-my-mind happy and excited. The next day, Saturday morning, I was aching from head to toe—but I forgot all about that when I saw the newspaper.

My name was all over it.

There are those before-and-after points in your life. I was great in the Bethel game and I knew it—more important, I discovered I could really play football. But it was right then, the instant I saw "LAWRENCE TAYLOR" in the paper, that something clicked inside. I knew then that I had arrived. For the first time I had a real sense of what I was sent here to do.

Even with all the hard work of learning the game, until that point in life I'd been more or less kicking around, having fun, getting away with things. I had lots of big dreams—I had told my mom when I was in junior high school that I was going to make a million dollars and buy her a big house—but I didn't have the first idea of how. So I focused on just having a good time.

Now things were different. Here was something I was good at, better than other people—and everybody knew it. And I had to take it seriously. This was a wake-up call.

After the Bethel game, my time on the bench was through. I was starting every game, playing better and better and playing with purpose. Even though I was the type who usually resisted instruction, I learned what I could from the Lafayette coaches, asked them about blocking, offensive schemes I had to look for and making defensive calls for the other guys. But I always did learn best from experience. The games taught me the most about what to look for, how to react. Most of all, they showed me how to get into the heads of the guys on the other side of the ball. I started to just *know* what they were going to do in a particular situation.

I kept on getting better in my senior year, too—and bigger. With a summer growth spurt on top of all the training, I got to be 6'1" and 207 lbs. Even played some offense—Coach Bucci had me playing tight end in a few games. I loved it—but more importantly, it helped me understand things better as a linebacker. Helped develop my sense of the timing of pass plays, my vision of the whole field and the instincts that have to come with that.

Everything was coming together to let me control what went on in games. The coaches knew that if they rushed me against the quarterback, something was probably going to happen.

Things were happening for me off the field, as well. Senior year was when I really started to put together the group of friends who have been my bedrock throughout the rest of my life. We called ourselves D'Fellas. There was Dylan Pritchett, John "J.D." Morning, Glenn "Cosmo" Carter, Eric Pruden and Eric Stone, the youngest. We all came together in different ways—but there had to be some past-life connection there or something.

Singing together, going on quadruple dates, playing cards, racing cars or just watching the trains go by, we were one tight unit.

And we've stayed that way. These guys helped me get through rehab a couple times. In fact, D'Fellas have always been there to anchor me to my roots and bring me back to myself when life has gotten too fast or too weird.

Meanwhile, I made the eastern regional team as defensive end. I even made all-state as tight end. As I started turning heads beyond Williamsburg, it was only a matter of time before I was going to have to deal with the issue of college.

Like I said, I'm not a big planner. Things have to reach out and hit me upside the head. I had never thought much about college. My folks had always wanted me to go so I could have a better life than they did, but I couldn't see where the money was going to come from—especially with my less-than-honors grades. Now that I was getting into the papers and making a name for myself, though, it seemed like somebody was going to offer me a football scholarship.

I was starting to get letters from some of the smaller schools. Coach Jones was doing his preacher's best trying to get some of the big colleges interested in me. That part of Virginia is a gold mine for football talent—in fact, NFL standouts Ron Springs and Mel Gray were my homeboys from Lafayette High—so big university teams do regular recruiting tours through there. Problem was, though, that I started playing so late in the game, that a lot of the bigger schools had been through there by the time I made my splash.

Well, something eventually did come from out of the blue: a big Cadillac with out-of-state plates. It drove up to Lafayette one day, and Coach Jones got paged to come out to meet a couple gentlemen: the defensive coordinator and recruiting guy for the University of North

Carolina. They asked him who he had who could play. Coach led them back to his office, slapped a 16-millimeter film onto the projector and started showing them my highlights.

After eight to ten minutes, they told him to turn it off.

"Coach, let's find this kid right now."

CHAPTER 02 | A Linebacker Is Born

Filthy McNasty and the Art of the Hit

I may have been a star at Lafayette High. I may have been All-State, made the Regional team.

But that didn't mean I was a football player yet. It didn't guarantee I was going to become one, either.

While the Lafayette team had maybe 35 people, there were over 100 players on the Tar Heels. Big guys—265, 280, 290 pounds. The All-ACC outside linebackers were both 230 and a good five inches taller than me. I was 205, 6'1". Big in Williamsburg—*real small* at Chapel Hill. Small…and about as important to the upperclassmen as the dirt between their cleats.

Right away I got that I wasn't gonna be rushed into anything. In fact, Bill Dooley, my first coach at UNC, was going to redshirt me for my whole freshman year. Couldn't figure out what to do with this small, raw guy. After watching me throw my body around in practice, though, he changed

his mind and started me out on special teams. Which meant I got to spend most of the year on the bench.

And that was fine with me. I knew I wasn't really ready for the college game, the mental part of it. From the playbook to the dynamics on the field, the college game was a hell of a lot more complex than high school football. Special teams let me spend time watching our All-ACC linebackers, Kenny Sheets and T. K. McDaniels. They had great moves, particularly Kenny. Maybe I was faster, maybe I was more aggressive, but Kenny *knew* so much. How to play the run, how to work around blocks, how to react to passing situations.

Playing special teams also meant I got to do what I did best: use my closing speed, sacrifice my body, go completely on instinct, play with total intensity—the kind of crazy, full-on, take-no-prisoners style I brought to the pro game.

Covering punts was what really got me noticed. I'd come right up the middle and try to block the kick. Never managed to do it—not once—but I'd flip right over the fullback and land on my head trying to get to that damn punter. The fans loved it! And when we were kicking, I'd go straight for the return man. I'd go around blockers, through 'em, under 'em, right over the top. Usually I'd end up right on my backside. But when I did get to the ballcarrier—watch out—I'd blast him, take him down, leap up and scream.

Back home, kids had called me "the Monster" just 'cause I was big. So this was my "Monster Cry." It sure as hell got the crowd going. My teammates loved it, too.

Meanwhile, Coach Dooley and the other coaches were deciding whether to put me on offense or defense. I liked both parts of the game

OK, but I always had the rather-hit-than-be-hit philosophy. Lucky for me, Al Groh and Jim Tressler, the UNC linebacker coaches, had spotted me. They saw I was fast, aggressive as hell, probably would grow and maybe had good instincts. They made me for an outside LB.

Foresight? Let's just say things worked out OK at that position.

Problem was the Tar Heels already had two great, All-ACC outside linebackers. So after that freshman year on special teams, I started sophomore year at inside linebacker. By this time I'd had a growth spurt—I was 6'3" and 230—and I felt ready to start. Broke a bone in my foot in the first game, though, and when I healed up they had me playing nose tackle. But I'm not a lineman. And I'm definitely not an inside guy—and even less of a nose tackle. Too much to think about, too many people coming at you and not enough room to move. Worse yet, I started to get shuffled around the field. Nose tackle, inside linebacker, outside linebacker—it was disorienting. And discouraging.

Another problem was that Coach Dooley left UNC at the end of my freshman year. His replacement, Dick Crum, had a real different style. Dools was a players' coach. We loved the guy. He understood that you treated ACC-Champion football players a little different than other students. Stuck his neck out for us more than once, in fact. Crum, now, he was a pretty hard case. He made the players toe the line, treated us like second-class citizens. He also threw out just about every part of Dooley's system. Call it rebuilding, call it going straight backwards—the fact was we went from ACC champs to a 5-6 season his first year.

With that, and getting moved to so many different positions, I was not a happy camper. I started to ask myself whether I was really developing, if I was ever going to make it as a football player.

I had started to build some strong friendships, though. That was keeping me sane. In my freshman year, I met Steve Streater, an All-ACC safety and punter and one of the best athletes on the team. From my freshman year until the middle of my senior year, I was rooming with him, running with him and partying with him. I've always been able to count on Steve for everything, and he's ended up being a lifelong inspiration. There was Paul Davis, another important guy in my life after Carolina—and Buddy Curry and Donnell Thompson and a bunch of other guys from Ehring House, the dorm where most of us football players lived.

These were my boys. I was lucky to have them, too. Because that same craziness that gave me an edge on the field was getting me into some dicey situations off of it. Let's just say I was playing hard, on and off the field.

There were fights. Bars that got trashed. Diving through the plastic back window of a guy's Jeep and chasing him out of his car. Climbing right back into my third-floor room at Ehring House—through the window. Yeah, we were all being crazy—defensive guys were supposed to be crazy.

But being me, I had to be *crazier*. My guys saved my butt from getting arrested and/or kicked out of school more than once.

I know when people think of me, they think of a lot of non-football stuff, the crazy stuff. A lot of it's true. It took me my whole college and pro careers, and a chunk of my retirement, to figure out what to do about the rocket that's always firing inside me, the itch I couldn't seem to scratch. Pretty much wherever I was, whatever I was doing, I've always had this urge to push things as far as I could make them go. But check this: the intensity that kept twisting my world into such wild shapes is the same thing that made me an All-American, All-Pro and NFL Hall of Famer. If it weren't for a couple of things that happened in the next year, though—one on the field and one off of it—that craziness probably would have twisted me right out of college, out of football and in a whole other direction.

As a junior I finally started at outside linebacker. For the first five games of the season, the results were nothing special—I was still getting used to playing there. Then came the North Carolina State game.

UNC-NC State is the big game down there, our Army-Navy, Cal-Stanford, Michigan-Ohio State. And that year, State was on its way to the ACC Championship for the first time ever. They were strong, they were at home, and the crowd was going wild. Late in the fourth quarter their team marched down the field looking to take away our thin 28-21 lead. Scott Smith, their quarterback, a guy who could pass and run, was killing us that day. As he took the ball from the center it looked like he was going to do it again.

He dropped back to pass.

Instinct took over—I went for him.

Let me tell you something. There's something about contact, feeling a guy crunching when you pop him, the snot coming out of his nose...it makes me feel alive. *There is nothing better in life than a violent, head-on collision.* It may not be your cup of tea, but it's what I was put here to do. It's that craziness, that intensity. It's who I am. My whole world came together in those moments—and it definitely came together in that one. Just as Smith's arm was going back, I smashed into him like a ton of bricks. The ball popped loose. We recovered, moved up the field and scored, shutting the door on them.

If there was one play that made our season, that was it. It was in the papers, on TV over and over again, and I couldn't go anywhere without people telling me what a great job I'd done. People started calling me "Filthy McNasty" because of my hard-hitting. Coaches started saying I could make it to the NFL. Hey, now!

Yeah, people had told me I was a good player before—but not like this. This was something special. It was like with that one play, *that one hit,* everything clicked. Now, for the first time, I got my answer: I had become a football player.

All I wanted to do was play the game, and play it really well. I started to understand what I could do as an outside linebacker. Maybe you could say that "LT" was born right there.

I mentioned there were *two* things that changed my life that year—and actually, they happened on the same day. After I got back from the NC State game, I went down to my favorite place to celebrate, which for me meant going totally out of control again. But as fate would have it, I ran into Linda instead.

Linda Cooley was gorgeous. But then there were lots of gorgeous girls in Chapel Hill-Durham. Linda had something different, something simple, pure and strong that really knocked me off my feet. The way she stood up to me and all my tough-guy swagger, for instance.

'Cause check this—I hadn't really figured myself out yet. Like the whole respect thing. I thought respect came from being the baddest dude on the block. Especially when I wasn't secure as a football player. I'd walk into bars, push people out of my way, beat on anybody who looked at me funny. And then after I became The Man, it got even worse—I had guys going ahead of me into the bar, clearing a path for me.

But Linda was not impressed. She saw right through it to the guy underneath.

She brought me down to earth. I started wanting to just hang out with Linda instead of going out and busting up joints.

Hey, I was still wild at heart. My act wasn't going to stop. Way too much buzzing inside for that. But Linda probably kept me from getting to the point of doing something so tough-guy and *stupid* that I'd be thrown out of school.

All in all, a good day. Now everybody knew I was a kick-butt football player—including me—and I'd met a very special lady. But there was the rest of the season to play.

I was going all out, having good games every week and loving it. Our whole team was doing well, in fact, and after a mediocre 1978 season we finished 1979 with an 8-3-1 record and went to the Gator Bowl in January. We played Michigan, who was heavily favored. They had All-conference and All-American guys like Anthony Carter, Curtis Greer and Butch Woolfolk—who would play with me on the Giants—as well as Mel Owens

"There is nothing better in life than a violent, head-on collision."

(Rams), Bubba Paris (49ers) and other future NFL players. I was fired up for that game; psyched, juiced, wired, spitting nails.

We played tough as a team and ended up getting the upset, 17-15, but I mostly remember that game as the *first* time I broke someone's leg.

Michigan QB John Wangler was running an option play, got ahead of his block—and found me. As they carried him off the field, he was trash-talking, saying he'd be back, but his leg was messed up bad—torn ligaments, cartilage, the works. John told me later that he thought that stuff was popping even before I hit him. Whatever—I guess the point is that guys just couldn't account for someone like me. I moved so fast, I covered the whole field from side to side like no one they'd ever seen. And as a junior, word wasn't really out about me yet. So Wangler was one of a bunch of guys who'd see me on the far side of the field and then suddenly find me right in their face.

I'd sure made an impression on our coaches—even Crum. In the off-season, they tweaked the defense, basically building it around me. I don't have to tell you I was looking forward to my senior year! North Carolina is known as a hoops school (ever heard of Michael Jordan?), but the football Tar Heels had started to get noticed. We were ranked #10 in the AP poll at the start of 1980.

We came out of the gate with a bang. Ripped through the first seven games. *Smothered* everybody on defense, allowing a total of two TDs and six field goals for that whole stretch. We jumped up to #6 in the polls. I was playing great. In our first game, Texas Tech looked like they were running the option. I pulled down the line, checked the fullback, saw he didn't have the ball, came back to the QB, saw the ball, hammered him, caused a fumble, recovered the fumble. The coaches called it a "trifecta."

Three weeks later it was our big rival, Clemson. We played them very tough. Clemson played us tough, too, and at the two-minute warning we were backed up on our 1-yard line with a skinny 24-19 edge.

OK, time to earn our lunch money.

First down, up the middle, no gain.

Second down, same thing.

Third down, Homer Jordan, the QB, rolls out for a play-action pass. Some guard forgets to pick me up, though, and I've got a clean shot at Jordan. I ring his bell for a nine-yard loss.

"It may not be your cup of tea, but it's what I was put here to do."

It's fourth down, defensive huddle, Steve Streater is screaming at us—the whole season is right here, right now, he says, we've got to strap it on. The snap—Jordan rolls right—and his pass to Jerry Gaillard goes wide out of the end zone.

Clemson comes away empty-handed and we run out the clock to get the win.

That goal line has become kind of a legend at UNC. But what mattered then was that we ended up with an 11-1 record, won the ACC Championship back and went on to the Bluebonnet Bowl, where we got a 16-7 win over Texas.

As for my season, I got 69 solo tackles, 16 sacks, and made All-America.

If there had been any doubts about me being a football player...

I found out later that there were some important NFL scouts at the Clemson game, guys from the Giants, the Cowboys, probably other teams as well. I was getting noticed. Being All-America didn't hurt, and my stats were great, but the intangible "big play" factor, that was what was drawing pro scouts to the games.

I spent most of the summer between my junior and senior years on campus. Me, Steve and some other guys roomed together. One afternoon this sharp-looking dude is standing at the door. He introduces himself, says his name is Ivery Black. He's an agent. Starts giving me his rap, how I've got a good chance of being picked first in the NFL draft, how he's got this plan to move me off campus into my own apartment so I can avoid any trouble (like, for instance, just about everything I'd been doing the last three years) and says he's going to lend me money and even cook for me.

What the...? Who *was* this dude?

I had just woken up from a nap—was I still dreaming?

But then he shows me the cash—that looks real enough—and the contract, and I think about it for about three seconds and say OK, yeah, sure, uh huh, the whole thing sounds pretty good to me.

Now, I had thought about the NFL, people had said I was draftable—but I'd given the actual process about as much thought as I gave most other crap that didn't involve putting quarterbacks on their behinds on Saturdays. Which is to say not a lot. I didn't know the politics of the draft or the strategy of getting a high pick. And I knew diddly about getting the best money.

More I think about how I made my way into the NFL, the more I'm amazed it happened at all. Yeah, I had the talent, and I shook it up in the right games, but it was like an unseen hand was getting me to the next stage in my career by putting people like Pete Babcock, Coach Jones, Al Groh, Jim Tressler and Ivery Black in front of me. The right people who got me to do the right thing at the right time. I was smart, but like a lot of young guys I was also such a fool about life...I can't help thinking how easy it woulda been to take even a little bit of a different direction and miss the whole boat.

A guy like Ivery, his expertise was in the life stuff department. Everything was laid out, bang, bang, bang. The plan was I'd move off campus in December, after the season. Once I did that, he moved into a hotel nearby, and yeah, he really did cook for me. Damn fine down-home cooking, in fact. Taught me to play golf, too.

The whole arrangement probably didn't completely square with NCAA policy, but then don't get me started on the NCAA. Their rules and regs, the whole thing about scholar athletes, it's all a bunch of crap. But I paid Ivery back every penny he'd loaned me, and over the years he's been a good friend, a good agent and a good advisor on all kinds of life stuff. And it's a safe bet he preserved my draft status, saving my sorry butt from some embarrassing episode or another.

Like I said, I'd had no idea about the draft when Ivery showed up, not least *where* I'd be drafted. But he was so sure of me, it was like he had insider information. And as the season unfolded, and I tore it up in games like Texas Tech, Clemson and the Bluebonnet Bowl, even I started to hear some of the buzz about me. I started seeing my name in the press as a possible early pick. Hmm…maybe this dude was right!

I started looking into the whole process more. I learned who was looking for what and who was interested in me. I learned that as far as defensive players went, I was sort of The Man in college ball. Bum Phillips, whose Saints had the number-one pick, might not take me. (He was looking for a power running back.) So that left the New York Giants. I knew their scouts had been out to look at some of my games.

Draft day. I'd been up pretty much all night partying with Steve, Donnell and some of the other guys who were probably going to go high in the draft, too. We'd been having some beers—more than just some—just kicking it and looking back at our time together as Tar Heels. Mostly, I think we were trying to cover up our nerves. I know I was.

The first pick went to the Saints. They took running back George Rogers out of South Carolina. OK, cool, not unexpected, no problem. I got up and stretched my legs, went to the kitchen, got a beer. I never heard the New York Giants select me as the second overall pick in the draft.

As the guys were congratulating me, Linda got me on the phone, told me to get my butt back to my place because Coach Ray Perkins was gonna be calling. I hustled back home and sure enough, there was Perk on the line, asking me if I could get up to New York City later that day.

As I threw some stuff in a bag, I thought to myself, son, things are starting to move *fast*.

Mind you, this is a kid from Lightfoot, Virginia, whose idea of a big city was Chapel Hill, packing for his first trip to the Big Apple. Fast? Let me tell you: I had no idea what fast was.

But I was about to find out.

Real fast.

Waking Up The Giants

Hunting Quarterbacks for a Friend

"I like to eat quarterbacks in the backfield."

There I was, the kid from backwoods Virginia facing the New York press—and handing them a load of fresh cow manure.

The Giants flew me up to New York as soon as I was drafted, and Ivery wrote me this speech for the press conference about how excited I was at being a New York Giant. I talked about Giant greats like Sam Huff and Rosey Grier and Andy Robustelli and probably a few others whose names I was reading for the first time.

Yeah, I was the Giants' #1 pick, but right now I was playing for my agents. Ivery and his partner Mike Trope were playing a whole other game to win over the press, the fans, Giants veterans and the Giants' money.

Even before draft day, some rumbling started coming from their vets. "Unnamed players" told the newspapers that the team didn't need me,

TAYLOR | By Lawrence Taylor

and that if they picked me up and paid me more than those guys were making, a lot of them were going to be leaving. When Ivery and Mike heard that, they sent Giants GM George Young a telegram in my name advising the team not to draft me. "It's a negotiating ploy," Ivery assured me. Scare the Giants. Make 'em cool down their vets, and get 'em ready for the kind of money we were going to be talking about. Something in the neighborhood of $750,000. More than any other guy on the team.

I had told Ivery and Mike that if they didn't get in the way of my football playing, I wouldn't get in the way of their negotiating. And I sure wasn't going to tell them to get me less money.

When we got to New York that day, Ivery told me all the right things to say and sent me out there to get the public on our side. He and Mike went in to talk brass tacks with Young. They got more or less what we wanted. And my act? The press ate it up. Everything was going according to plan. Two down. Time to tackle the veterans.

But first, something else almost tackled me and knocked me out of the game.

Late one night during my rookie camp I got a call from Ivery. He told me he had some bad news. Steve Streater had broken his neck in a car accident.

I had been out partying half the night and I was drunk and sleepy, but once Ivery got through to me who he was talking about and what had happened, I was making plans to get back to North Carolina the next morning.

Talk about a change in perspective. Here it was, my first NFL training camp, a place I'd sweated blood for six years to get to—and I was steaming out the door as soon as the sun came up. Some Giants staffer asked where

CHAPTER 03 PAGE 47

"Back in training camp, I was all business. I was on a mission from God."

I was going, tried to get me to talk to Head Coach Ray Perkins, but I just straight-armed him out of my way. "Screw football," I said. That was where my mind was at.

I knew Steve was messed up pretty bad. I tried to suck it up, to be cool, to be strong for him. But I could not have prepared myself for what he actually looked like when I walked into his hospital room. There was this metal halo thing around his head with bolts screwed right into his skull, like something out of a science fiction movie. And what you could see of him was just lying there like a corpse. The doctor told me Steve had been asking for me. Then he whispered that Steve was going to be paralyzed. For life.

So what did I do? I went off on the doctor. All the shock and anger and sadness and fear I was trying to hide came out in one big explosion. I pushed him into the corner like a blocking sled, practically beat on the man, screaming at him. *If he was the damn doctor why couldn't he do something?* Then I went off on Steve.

"Get up! This is not you! You *got to get up!*"

Eventually they got me calmed down, but that was it. I was done. Here was my boy, a beautiful football player, a maniac who could win games on his will alone—someone who was just so *alive*—and he had been taken down in an instant. I felt completely broken up. I felt like I'd lost Steve. Suddenly nothing made any sense. I'd been on a high about my success, career, #1 draft choice, New York City, big money...and now I was getting a real serious lesson in how quickly everything could turn to dust.

What was the point?

I stayed with him in his room that day, that night and most of the next day. It was the lowest point in my life that far. I've been through some unbelievably bad times since then, but that's still one of the worst. I just sat in that hospital room, and when I wasn't crying or feeling like crap, I was talking with Steve and telling him what was going through my mind, that football didn't matter to me anymore. And the dude was so strong, here he was paralyzed, neck broken, career over, life blown apart— he starts straightening *my* head!

The main thing he got through was this: he couldn't play football, so I had to play for him. I had to get myself together, wipe the snot off my nose, go back to New York and *make it happen.*

Steve was like my brother. I would do anything for him. So if I couldn't make him get up and walk no matter how loud I yelled, then dammit, I had to have a kick-butt season for him. *That* was the point!

I dedicated my whole first year with the Giants to him. Then I got the next plane back to New York.

Steve is doing great today, by the way. He's been paralyzed from the waist down since that day but is real mobile in his wheelchair. Gets a hell of a lot done as the director of the North Carolina chapter of Students Against Drunk Driving. I get down there for promotional events when I

can. He's still one of my best friends. I'm just one of a lot of people he keeps fired up with his courage.

Back in training camp, I was all business. I was on a mission from God.

Even from the first rookie minicamp, I was making the kind of kamikaze plays I'd been doing basically since high school—smacking blockers, jumping and flipping over guys, taking down ballcarriers in the backfield. I was practicing at full speed—just being me, in other words. I ran speed drills right alongside the DBs and receivers and kept up with them, and in our scrimmages I was making sacks and causing fumbles. The coaches were discovering what everyone else in the NFL was about to find out—that you had to do a lot more than throw a running back at me if you wanted to keep Lawrence Taylor from the QB.

I went from fourth team to second team to first team pretty quickly. The veterans could see I had speed and moves. I had four sacks, recovered a fumble and caught a runner in the backfield in my very first scrimmage. I got from one side of the field to the other like no one they'd seen before.

But I wasn't exactly winning any popularity contests. There were some exceptions—Harry Carson, the middle linebacker who would join me in the Hall of Fame in 2006, had even made a point of taking me out to dinner when I showed up in New York that first time. Most of the vets, though…well, they were less than room temperature to the rookie.

Whatever. Since getting back from Steve's hospital room, the battle to win them over just didn't seem worth the effort anymore. They could think what they wanted. I just kept my head down and focused on learning the defense.

I knew who I was, and I knew I could play. No doubt there were some solid players on the team, studs like Harry or Brad Van Pelt who even *I*

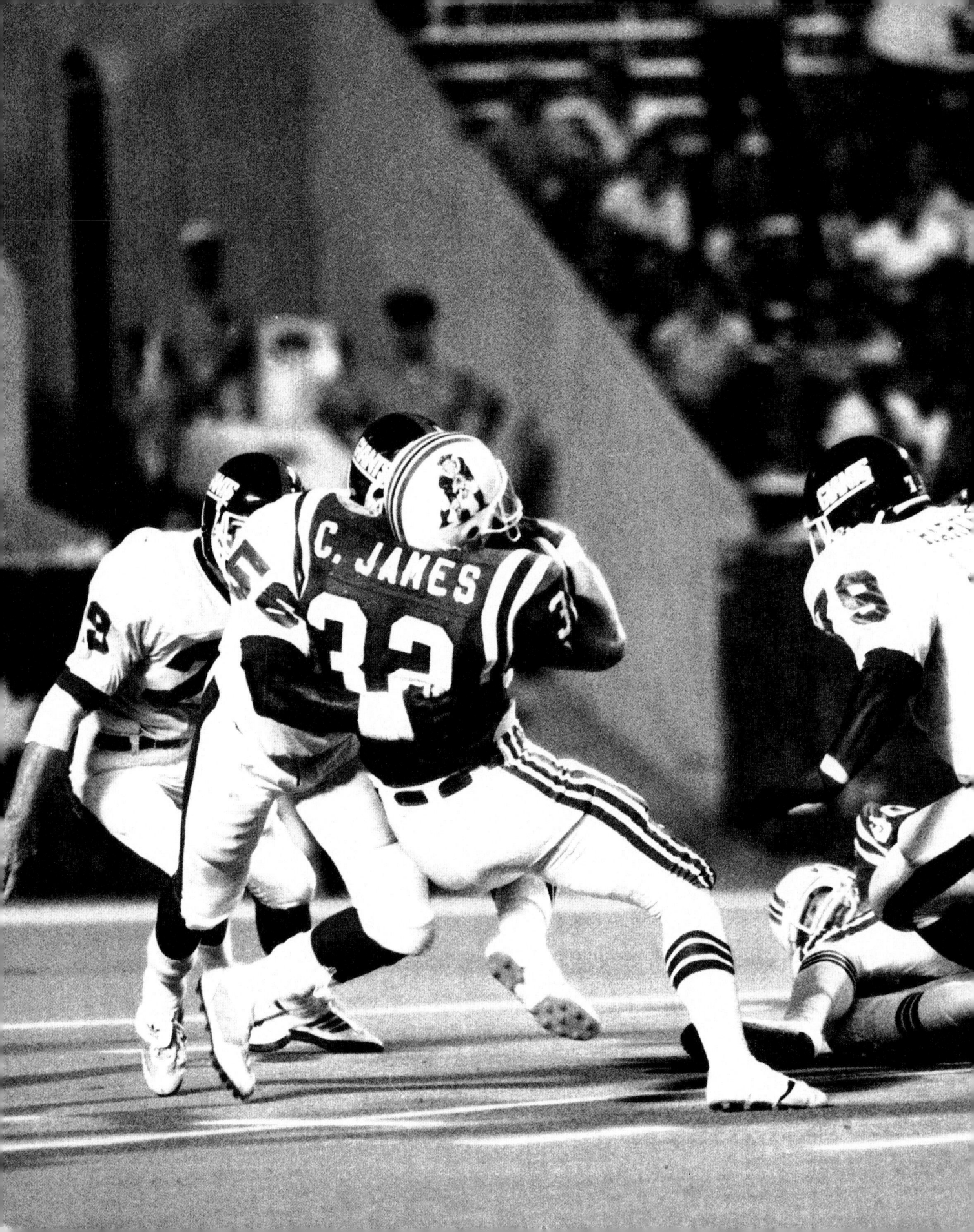

had heard of, but I definitely felt like I was at least as good as they were. And anyway, who were these guys to say the team didn't need me? The Giants were 4-12 the year before, 27th out of 28 NFL teams in points allowed. They'd gone 21-41 in the last four seasons. Not exactly setting the world on fire.

And I was playing for Steve, not them. So if they didn't like me, fine. Just stay out my way.

That was the idea, anyway. But I didn't plan for a Mr. William Parcells. Bill was the defensive coordinator under Perkins. Talk about karma—we were ragging on each other from practically the first day. He'd tell me I was tipping the blitz, getting fooled by the play-action...or just plain clueless.

"Son, you're just like a ball in high grass. Do you know what that is?"

"No, Coach..."

"Well, I'll tell you: LOST."

Thing is, though, I used to give it right back, tell him where he could get off. Come on, I was earning more than he was! The outside linebacker I'd taken the starting job from was named John Skorupan. One hot afternoon when Bill had pushed me over the limit with his damn needling and picking, I yelled at him from across the field: "Listen, you either cut me, trade me or put Skorupan back in...but just get off my back!"

Looking back, that was kind of a stupid thing to do. Coach Perkins or George Young or anyone else in the front office might have said, "Fine with us, kid," and cut me. As it was, though, the field just went quiet. People didn't talk back to coaches like that. (Not back then, at least...though you're seeing more of it now. Another way I changed the game?)

Well, Parcells, he didn't say anything more. He kept after me in more sly ways over the years, but right then he learned I had a mean streak. And he liked it.

Check this, though: I'd told Bill in training camp, "Coach, I want to be the best one who ever played this game."

And he knew I could be. That's why he was always riding me. He said straight out that he was putting extra pressure on me to make sure I could face the pressure in game situations.

Probably Bill's biggest gripe with me was my inability to learn the playbook. Like every NFL team, the Giants had this huge, eight-pound playbook—and we were supposed to know it cold. Now, the defense was

"I was spending so much time in offensive backfields, they were like my personal playground."

shifting from a 4-3 the year before to a 3-4, so everybody was learning at least some of the playbook again, but it's like memorizing the phone book if you're looking at one of these bad boys for the first time. You want to get a sense of the mental game of football? Try to memorize hundreds of formations, line-of-scrimmage calls and stunts with names like "Green Read," "Stack," "Fire," "Loop" and "Mustang." And do it in a few weeks—well enough to execute 'em with split-second timing against 300-plus pound guards.

That damn book was like a ball and chain for me. Took me three years to learn it. And I'm not dumb. I could figure out from a few tiny clues exactly how a play was going to go down, and then know just what to do. A regular Sherlock Holmes. And my recall was outstanding: you got by me with some move once, good luck using it ever again, boy. But that kind of learning happens on the field, in the moment, and at speed. Learning some set plays from a book? I just wasn't very interested. Not how I liked to do things. But it was how the Giants did things. And Bill was there to remind me of that every time I missed a play.

I got called out in practice. I got called out in games. I got called out by Bill, by Coach Perkins, by veteran players. In the locker room, in front of 75,000 people, on national television, in the newspapers.

Our first exhibition game that season was an away game against Chicago. I was completely pumped up, adrenaline pounding through my veins, literally shaking.

But then I always do that. Ten years later it was still the same nerves business with me.

They put me in for the first half, watching how their investment was going to perform in a game situation. I had a lot of tackles; I sacked Vince

Evans and whoever else they put out at quarterback. Coach Perkins said he was real pleased with the way I played. But then he went and told a reporter, "Lawrence made a couple of errors that cost us."

Those errors were mostly named Walter Payton.

Number 34 gave me some expensive rookie lessons on how to set yourself up for a running attack. He'd do that weird, midair Bambi stride move he had and *boing* he was gone. Well, I filed that stuff away. Next time I played him, I'd be looking for it.

Preseason was going OK for me. I was making some good plays and I was getting some buzz going. I made four out of the seven preseason sacks we got. I was beginning to cut down on mistakes, too...ah, well, I was still making tons of mistakes—but I was making 'em at full speed. I was learning how to turn "mistakes" into "big plays"—my specialty.

Take for instance my very first regular season game. We were playing the Eagles at home. Philadelphia was just coming off a Super Bowl year, and the Giants hadn't beaten them since '75. That was motivation enough for me. I felt like I was going to turn this whole thing around single-handedly! As it happened, their defense was firing on all cylinders and we ended up losing 24-10, but overall we played a very tough, physical game. I think they could see the Giants weren't a guaranteed win anymore.

I know I gave them something to remember us by: I had my first sack, the first of my many memorable meetings with Ron Jaworski. It was also one of my first successful "mistakes."

The way the play was set up, I was supposed to check Harold Carmichael, their big wide receiver. He went in motion, but then when he turned around and came back, rookie LT was way out of position. Oops. My bad. Now what? Well, I'd developed a rule of thumb early on: when in doubt, rush the QB and knock him on his butt.

There was some fullback there to protect Jaworski, but blocking backs were like flies to me, son. I swatted him away and closed in on Jaworski, who was just about to pass.

I had this tackling style I'd developed at North Carolina. In the pros I started making it into an art. What I'd do is, first, plow into the guy from his blind side. Plant my helmet in his back if I could. With my left arm, I'd wrap his torso good and tight. The right arm, that's the beauty part: I'd have it up high as I made contact and, just as he's about to throw, bring it down on him like a steam hammer. Do it right and it'd be like I stuck his finger into a light socket. Often enough, dude would let go of the ball. I could mess up his passing without doing another thing: he'd be hearing footsteps the rest of the game. And that's exactly what happened with Jaworski.

When we played the Eagles again in November, all I had to do was wink at old Ron and he was practically peeing his pants. He was looking around to see where I was, rushing his passes, doing his part to make the Eagles lose to us for the first time in six years. Damn, I got into Jaworski's head so bad, he was hearing footsteps the rest of his career.

But in that first game, along with my first sack, I got my first penalty. Unnecessary roughness.

I came back to the sideline, pissed off at the refs. That was a clean hit! Hard, but clean. I always played clean, even though I had this superbad image. I figured if I made good, hard contact I didn't need to waste time on cheap stuff. Still, I figured Coach Perkins was going to tee off on me. Dumb rookie missed his assignment and then gave up fifteen yards.

He looked at me and just said, "I don't care if you get a hundred penalties like that, you just keep tackling that way."

After losing three of our first five games that year, the Giants started putting together some wins, and it was the defense that was making it happen. We were starting to believe in ourselves. The fans were starting to believe, too. "The Giants are for real," the papers said after we beat the Falcons 34-27 in a key overtime game. That game was where we really started to gel on defense.

I took one of the Falcons' running backs out of the game—a guy named Lynn Cain who had leveled me with a submarine block near the end of regulation. At the end of the next play, he was on a stretcher.

Steve Streater was in the house to see me do it, too. What a feeling! We had pulled out a victory, we were playing as a team and I had dished out some monster hits. All in front of the friend I'd dedicated my season to. I had a limo bring Steve back to the Giants' hotel after the game. It was good to see him looking so strong. We hung out and kicked it like old times.

The Giants continued to improve as a team. We were starting to win…at least more than we were losing. We were coming together on the field and finding chemistry off of it. People were having fun, laughing, partying together. Stuff you didn't see much of when you were 4-12. And I was right in the middle of it. Guys had seen that I was serious about football and about winning, and they respected that. But I think it was my playful, good-time personality that started to work on hard cases like Brad Van Pelt.

After a while, Brad and Brian Kelley were buying me drinks and introducing me around at some kickin' parties.

And on the field, we kept winning. Took three of four toward the end of the season. People could talk playoffs without getting laughed out of the locker room.

Check this: our offense was ranked at or near the bottom of the league. They were doing what they could, no doubt. But Phil Simms had been out with a separated shoulder, and we had no running game to talk about.

It was our *defense* that totally rocked. And I was the boot. After terrorizing quarterbacks every week, word started getting around the league about me—that there was basically no stopping the Giants' rookie linebacker on a pass rush. I was getting into the coaches' heads just like I'd gotten into Jaworski's. They were starting to plan games around me, moving tight ends and blocking backs around. But nobody came up with anything that worked.

Me, I was just doing my thing. I was having fun and trying to learn the defense. Perkins and Parcells were the ones seeing the bigger picture. It took them as long as the first game to get what I could do in a game situation. And when they saw other coaches making this strategic shift, they started to give me a little more rein. Parcells and Perkins were even talking about letting me rush every single play! They had to admit that a lot of my "mistakes" were paying off.

"He's still making mistakes," Perk told a reporter. "But he can make mistakes and still make the play. He makes things happen." Well, duh! Thing was, I could see things on the field that made a lot more sense than what some diagram in a playbook said I should do.

Like this: against the Cardinals in the second-to-last game of the season, there was a pass play where I was supposed to be dropping into coverage. But we had them backed up against their end zone—and what I saw was *sack, fumble, score.* So I came in like a bullet, tossed the tight end to the ground and ran into Neil Lomax at full speed. Lomax crumpled and the ball came loose. I was lucky to play with guys who were heads-up enough to keep up with my freelancing—our defensive end, George Martin, picked it up and ran it in for the TD.

Bill told me that play wasn't in the playbook. I told him. "Well, Coach, you better put it in there Monday."

After the Cardinals game we were legitimate contenders. We had one last must-win game between us and the playoffs: Dallas.

You didn't just walk over the Cowboys. Dallas was America's Team, with NFL rushing leader Tony Dorsett, the Doomsday Defense and a whole lineup of future Hall of Famers. But we were able to keep the score close the entire time. Our defense was shutting them down just about every way we could. They did a good job blocking me, and I was pretty quiet most of the game...but I'm about the big plays. The only thing better than a bone-crushing, snot-popping hit is doing it when it can turn the game around. That's showtime for me!

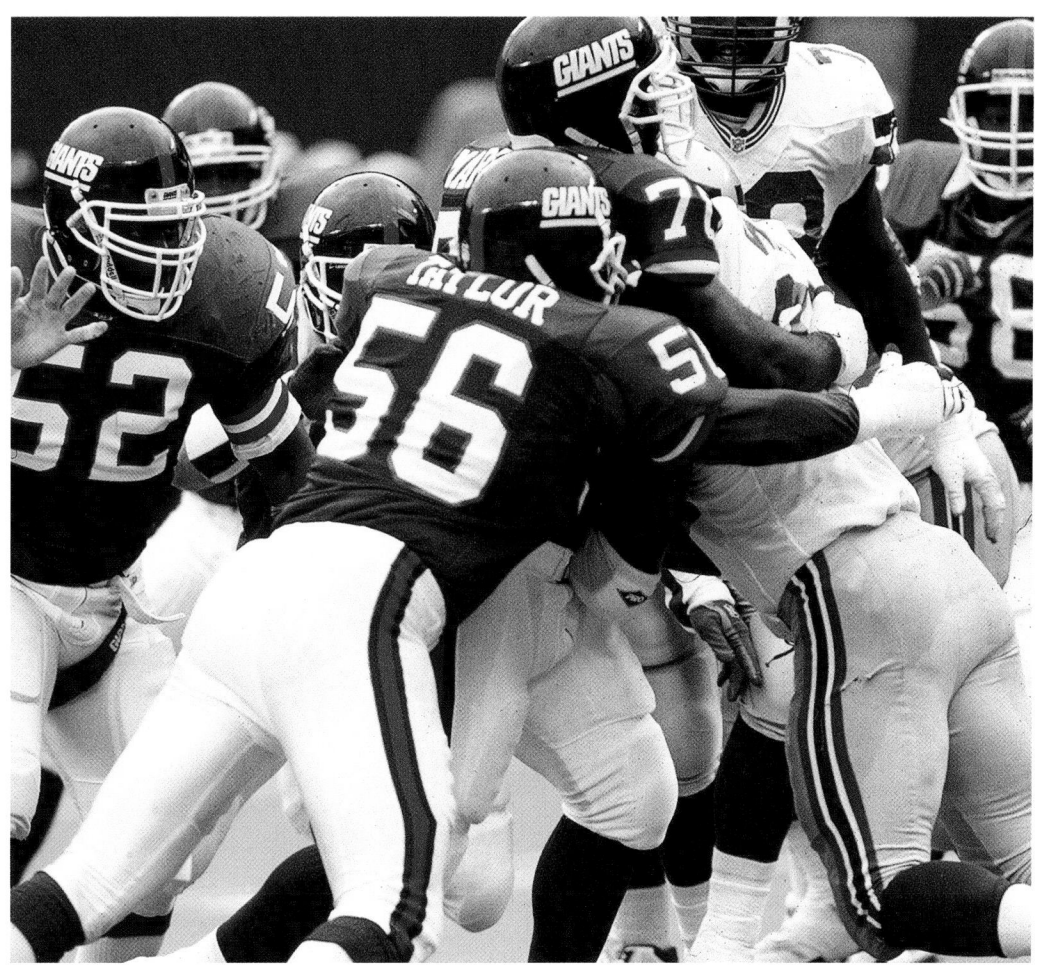

We'd gone into overtime, the score tied 10-10. Danny White pitched out to Dorsett. But it was an ugly toss, and Dorsett didn't have control. He was just getting hold of it when I landed on his back, knocked the ball loose and then recovered it. That set up a kick. Sure thing, I thought—I'd won the game for us! But the wind blew our field goal into the upright. Damn! Gotta do it again. So three plays after we turned the ball over to Dallas, I paid another visit to their backfield. I came after White like he'd stolen something from me. He got rid of the football, tossing it in the general direction of Drew Pearson—and my roommate Byron Hunt intercepted it. This time, we were able to convert the field goal and win the game, which *almost* put us in the playoffs. But first we'd need the Jets, of all teams, to take out the Packers the next day.

So on Sunday we all came out to the stadium to watch the game and root for the Jets. (There's a first time for everything, right?) Our crosstown rivals did not let us down. We were going to the playoffs!

For my teammates, especially the veterans, it was deeply emotional, it was redemption, it was salvation. Likewise for the fans. They hadn't had a playoff team since 1963. The last time they had had a winning team to root for was 1972! So I had to respect that. I liked being able to help make that happen for them. But coming off a Bowl winner at North Carolina, it wasn't enough for me. I wasn't going to be satisfied until we'd been to the mountaintop.

Our first playoff game was against Philadelphia. We took care of business, beating them 27-21. I had a great game on defense and also special teams: I forced one fumble on the Eagles' first punt return and then another on a kickoff return—both of which turned into scores for us.

After that it was on to San Francisco for the NFC semifinals. We played them with everything we had, but they had that much more. The 49ers were on their way to the Super Bowl that year and were not to be denied. It was a hard loss—38-24—and I was so ticked off about it that I ended up taking it out on the press. I avoided 'em and avoided 'em, but they kept after me and I finally just teed off on 'em. Another rookie mistake.

Once I calmed down, though—on a beach in Hawaii—I realized that, all things considered, I had had a rookie year for the ages. I was voted Rookie of the Year and Defensive Player of the Year. I may not have been going to Detroit for the Super Bowl, but here I was, about to play in the Pro Bowl. I'd had a great season for my friend Steve, who was in my heart every week. And I came through on my pledge: I had eaten exactly nine and a half quarterbacks in the backfield.

Not too bad. Especially since, like the song says, I did it my way. I'd played at full speed, using my instinct more and more. In some cases I had dictated how games turned out. I'd had fun, too. Hey, I was spending so much time knocking people around in NFL offensive backfields, they were like my personal playground.

But then they had to go and put up guards to keep me out…

The Honeymoon Is Over

Chess Games in the Trenches, a Changing of the Guard

My rookie season was so good it was unfair.

What I mean is, everything went so right that first year I almost got to expect that that's the way it would be from now on. Winning, going to the playoffs, the D tight and having fun. Perk guiding the whole show with that quiet, intense style and thousand-yard stare. And oh yeah, all those easy sacks...

One thing I was learning in my young life, though: change is inevitable. And changes began to pile on, one on top of another, with me trying to hold on to the ball at the bottom of the heap.

First, I had a nice off-season in Carolina and finally got hitched to Linda. I'd proposed to her the year before, with less planning and style than I'd showed sacking Ron Jaworski: while we were driving back from the airport one day, I tossed her the ring in a box and said, "Here."

Romantic, huh? She said yes anyway, the first of a lot of wonderful things she'd do for me in spite of me being a less-than-perfect husband. Marrying her was one of the better decisions I ever made. I doubt she'd say the same thing.

Linda had given me a beautiful gift, my son T.J., who'd come along in August.

After reconnecting with my roots, spending time with my mom and pop and then with Steve and some of my other Tar Heel boys, it was back to work. Training camp, preseason games.

And that's where the first little hiccup hit me.

Turf toe. It's a small break or bruise on the toe bone, I mean tiny...but nagging.

Looking back on it, that toe seems like the first little crack in the rosy picture I had of life in the NFL.

The toe ended up slowing me down for weeks. And after that I sprained my knee. Had to wear one of those metal braces between games. Couldn't practice. The most playing time I missed was a half a game, but that was a very, very big deal to me. Because my principle is if you can walk, you can play, simple as that.

Football's violent; people get hurt and people play hurt. Next time you see a game, *listen* to it! *Wham! Crunch!* You *know* there's pain on every single play.

And I didn't ever want to sit out with some pissant toe or knee sprain or hangnail, because the team needed me. This book is filled with things that happened—sacks, runners stuffed for a loss, fumbles, interceptions, defensive touchdowns—whole games we won *because I was playing*. Because I was on the field, messing up the other team. But I most always had some

kind of thing going on in some part of my body. Hell, all football players do. That's why their lifespans are twenty years shorter than the average person's. You don't believe me? Look it up. Yeah, they've got studies that just blame it on weight. And being as big as some of those offensive linemen can not be good for you, sure, but I don't have to be a scientist to tell you the real reason. It's the damn *pounding* you take. Your whole body gets seriously abused in football—your muscles, your bones, your guts.

"There's one sure way to fire me up to do something...

Tell me I can't."

Excuse me for getting off the story. I'm just trying to paint a picture for you here, give you an idea of what an NFL career means. It's something to think about the next time you and your buddies are posted up on the sofa watching a game. I want you to get a sense of how *intense* the game is with all that pain—and why winning and losing matter so much, and why all the crap that came down in '82 and '83 almost made me want to chuck the whole thing.

Along with the injuries that were starting to become a factor my second year, along with every other player in the NFL I suddenly had to deal with another, bigger issue: a players' strike. Some labor issues that we'd been talking about with the league since 1981 had come to a head after the second game of the '82 season, and the NFL Players Association felt the only thing it could do was get us off the field. The issue was basically protecting the little guys, the lower-paid players, from getting chewed up and spit out by the owners. (For me, I agreed with the principle so I stuck with the guys, even though I had my own views on the fight they chose to pick and how they went about it.)

Everybody thought it was just going to be for a few days—the strike ended up lasting eight long weeks. Now, you take a guy born to be a football player, an aggressor, someone who's got an itch to hit and live life fast, and you make him hang around the house for most of the season— losing money the whole time. That's a *recipe* for nastiness, my friend. Let's just say it was not a good time for me, and *definitely* not good for Linda.

Eventually the league and the NFLPA straightened out their differences and we got back to playing. My first game back was against Washington. I was slow, still feeling my knee situation, still feeling the time away from the game and all the sitting around that came with it. I didn't do nothing in that game. The press was whispering, "What happened to Lawrence Taylor?" Writing about sophomore slumps, mortality, all that.

Next week, after a short rest, we played Detroit on Thanksgiving. That game featured one of my only bright memories from 1982 and 1983. In fact, it's one of my favorite memories of my whole career. It's the play that probably introduced me to fans across the nation. New York knew about me, and so did other NFC East cities. But Thanksgiving Day you know every guy in the whole country is kicking back, burping up turkey and watching football.

I started the game on the bench. That was Bill's decision—he said my knee and foot were slowing me down. The call did not go down well with me. You know how I feel about sitting because of injuries. I knew I could play. I knew I could always come up with something special. So there was some unpleasant language over the issue. But Bill was the defensive coordinator, not me. So my roommate Byron Hunt started at outside linebacker. Bill said depending on how the game went he'd probably send me in later. But I was sulking.

"If you're not going to let me start," I told Bill, "then forget you. I don't want to play."

Well, early second quarter, he told me to get out there. *Yes!* I think I was on the field and in the defensive huddle before he finished saying "there." They had to remind me to put my helmet on.

Talk about making up for lost time. First I stripped the ball from running back Billy Sims. Harry Carson recovered and we got a field goal out of it, which put us on the board. A couple of possessions later, I had a big sack, collaring the Lions' QB, Gary Danielson, and tossing him down on the turf like in a Western movie brawl. (I was into Westerns. Used to do that little shoot-em-up move after big hits until they told me to cool it. Man, the NFL—the No Fun League.)

Okay, fourth quarter now, score's tied, and the Lions are on our four-yard line on third down. Looks like they're gonna score. Can't let that happen now, can we? It's a tight situation, but I'm starting to have fun again, to feel the game, to think it. And when I look over at the offensive set, *bam*. I know what I'm looking at.

Now check this: there's this idea of me as a shoot-from-the-hip guy who never knew what defense we were in, didn't know the playbook, made it up as he went along—who basically improvised his way into the Hall of Fame. There's something to that, OK. And yeah, I've helped push that image. But I also played a serious mental game. I did my damn homework, keeping detailed records (in my head) of just about every play that had ever been run at me.

So when I saw the Lions splitting their backs, I recognized that right away. It was another team that had used it, in fact—the Packers, on a Monday night game earlier that year. The play was really designed to set me up. Horace King, one of the Lions' backs, was going to go out for a pass. He'd run right at me so that if I cut to the outside, he'd go inside, and if I went inside, then, you guessed it, he was going to go out. When the Packers had used that play with Jim Jensen, I'd been burned for a TD. But you don't fool LT twice, son. Once I sussed the play out, I knew just what I was going to do. It was part of a defensive scheme set up for just that play. Brian Kelley, the inside linebacker (a super-smart guy with a computer-type brain when it came to storing sets and schemes), would cover the receiver if he went inside, and also pick up the tight end if the play went to him. That left me to work the outside, the part of the field where I could really do my thing.

Sure enough, at the snap King came straight at me. The tight end started to slant to the inside, and I took a step or two as if I was going to follow him toward the middle. Danielson bit, and looked outside to King. I could tell Danielson had already crossed me off his list and wouldn't be looking for me anymore. That's when I started to move toward King. I had the thing so completely covered mentally, I knew where King was going to make his cut, and where the ball was going to be. I was moving there before Danielson even threw it. Perfect timing! I stepped in front of King—excuse me, my man—caught that bad boy, and I was off down the sideline. I passed right by Bill along the way, who was screaming at me, *"Run! Run! Run!"*

Don't need to tell me that, Coach, I'm running for my life, trying to outrun this Lions guy who's shadowing me the whole way. And as I got near the goal line, I looked back and saw that it was...oh, my shadow.

I didn't have a fancy TD move, so I nearly took my knees off trying to improvise one, sliding into the end zone. It ended up being a 97-yard INT return, the third longest in Giants history. What mattered, though, was that it ended up winning the game for us, 13-6.

There's one sure way to fire me up to do something. Tell me I can't.

Bill never benched me against my will again.

Like I said, that was the highlight. 'Cause the rest of the season wasn't much to write home about. We finished 4-5.

But if we thought *that* was a comedown from 9-7 and the playoffs, it was gonna get a lot worse.

A while after the Detroit game, Coach Perkins announced he was going to leave at the end of the season to go coach the Crimson Tide at Alabama. That was a shocker. I respected Perk. He was damn serious about winning and he treated me fair. But while I didn't like seeing Perk go, I was happy about Bill Parcells taking over. Like I said, Bill and I got each other. We busted each other's chops a lot, but he knew what to do with me. And I liked playing for him. Fact is, I might not have stuck around for anybody else over the next year.

Now, Bill's a good coach. He's got two Super Bowls to prove it. I wouldn't be surprised to see him win another one with Dallas, either. But even the best coach can only be as good as his players. What he inherited from Perk was a team that, in spite of our good season in '81, was going downhill. There were some changes Bill should have made when he took over as head coach, particularly on offense, and didn't. Not quick enough, anyway. We ended up going 3-12-1 in 1983. We couldn't produce. We'd go into games and *not even have a chance* to win.

The problem was simple: the offense. They just could not score. They couldn't even hold on to the ball—which the defense eventually decided was fine: we felt like we could score more points than the offense, anyway. Keep those dogs on the bench! At least the defense could really take it to the other team, put some hurt on them. The offense could basically only hurt itself. It's easy to blame Scott Brunner, our quarterback. He'd done good things the year before but was in way over his head this year, like he'd gone backward. There was plenty of blame to go around, though. Receivers, backs, O-line. You win as a team, and you lose as a bunch of underperforming, messed-up units.

I learned to get past the John Ayerses of the world, the big guards, by basically hitting them as hard as I could—which in my case was real hard. That would stop the guy's momentum when he was pulling. And if I could knock his hands out of the way, that's pretty much all I needed to do. No momentum, no hands, no problem—I'd be past him and on my way to the quarterback. I also learned to work with teammates, linemen like Leonard Marshall, kicking guards and tackles inside so my guys could go around them for the sack.

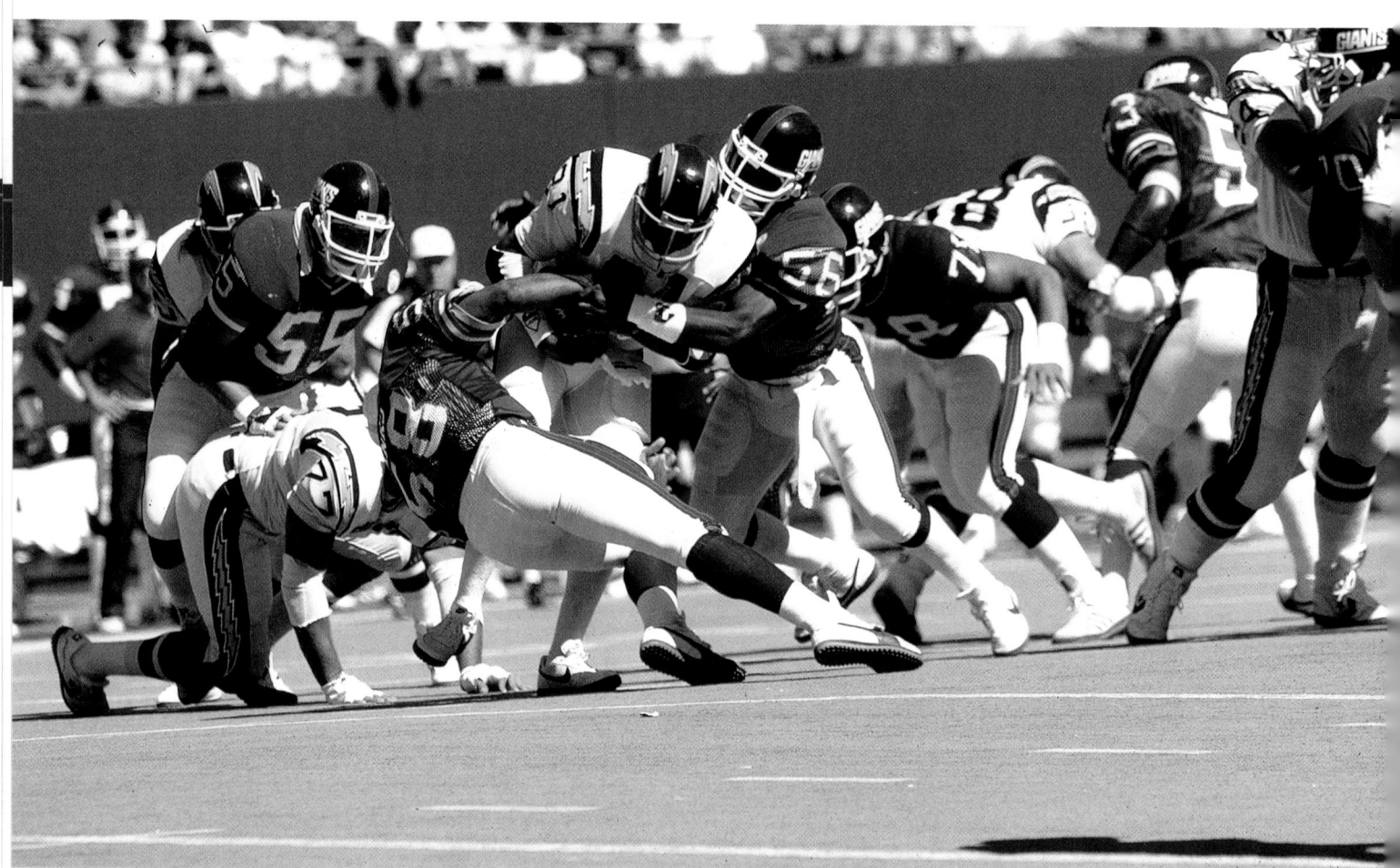

With double-teams, I learned you can usually exploit the differences between the two guys who are working on you. See, one is usually taking a back seat compared to the other one, who is doing most of the beating. So if you can stun the enforcer—usually a tackle or guard—with a double slap and an uppercut, you'll have the split second you need to slip inside ahead of the other dude.

There were some other moves I learned, too, but basically it all involved adding more technique and mental preparation to my basic, instinct-oriented game. I had been such an animal, making things happen by just throwing myself into each play at full speed, that this *technique* business was a strange new thing for me. In the long run, though, it saved a lot of wear and tear. And, I got to say, it made me a better player.

And none of it would have happened unless the changes in blocking forced me to change too.

So maybe change wasn't always such a bad thing.

Here's my final thought on the blocking issue: if I wanted it bad enough, nobody really ever came up with an effective scheme to stop me. I may sound arrogant, but I'm just stating the facts.

I'll show you what I mean. Check this play from that '83 Redskins game: second quarter, Theismann is back to pass, I'm blitzing from the right side. Joe Jacoby, their 300-pound tackle, slides over to block me. I grab him by the shoulder pads and just throw the dude. Theismann sees me and starts running out of the pocket. Now George Starke, the right tackle (another 260 pounds of Hog), comes back in to pick me up. By that time I got plenty of momentum and I just shove him down without slowing. I get Theismann 15 yards downfield. And he runs a 4.6.

But I'm LT.

''Everyone should watch out. My back is to the wall, and everything will be different.''

That's Parcells at the beginning of the '84 season. And he meant every word. Bill knew he had barely survived to see 1984 after we stunk up the place the year before. No loyalty now, no sentimentality, it was past time for some housecleaning. Offensive deadbeats were flying out the door, including Brunner and most of our stone-handed wide receivers.

That was a good thing. The problem was, defensive guys were going with 'em.

Brad Van Pelt, traded to Minnesota. Brian Kelley, traded to San Diego. Cornerback Terry Jackson was sent to Seattle. And Beasley Reece, my man back at safety—they waived him before the '83 season was out. These were my boys, the heart of the Giants D, the only thing that worked right on the team!

Add to that Harry Carson out of camp on a contract holdout, and I was one pissed-off linebacker. There was a serious chill between Bill and myself, and a war of words in the newspapers. Bill said Harry (who was the team captain now that Kelley was out) should look up the definition of "leadership." I came back and said Parcells should look up the definition of "honesty."

I was stepping up, taking more of a leadership role with Harry out—even if I wasn't really being completely honest myself. I had just let Donald Trump give me $1 million to play for his USFL team, only for Ivery Black and Mike Trope to have the Giants buy my contract back. I was now one of the highest-paid defensive players in the NFL. Some people called it extortion. I called it taking care of my family.

Harry came back, Bill and I moved on and we had a pretty good preseason. I was still down about Brad, Brian, Beasley and the other guys, but Harry counseled me that I was going to see a lot of people let go if I stuck around in the NFL. And you know what? By the time they waived my boy Pepper Johnson in '93, even though it felt like they'd ripped my left arm off, I was the one telling the rest of the team that we had to move on.

Some of the new people Parcells had brought in before the '84 season looked like they might amount to something—even some of the new defensive guys, like linebackers Carl Banks and Gary Reasons. We started the season by winning two in a row against Philly and Dallas. After winning just one out of our last twelve games the season before, that tasted sweet. As for me, I came out of the gate like a freight train. Eight sacks in the first four games.

Maybe things were looking up. Fact was, although it would take two years to see it happen, that with all these changes Parcells had started to put together a team that could make the long climb to the Super Bowl.

But I was going to have to take a few detours to get there with them.

Brothers In Arms

And a Few Giant Pains in the...

An Army of One.

If that military recruiting slogan had been around when I was playing, some people would have used it to describe my style of play. Freelancing, doing whatever I felt like, attacking on my own. There's a lot of truth to it, but if anybody thought I wasn't really a team player, that I put myself first, didn't pay attention to what my teammates were doing, well, that was BS.

Yeah, I did make sure I got paid what I deserved. And yeah, I got preferential treatment from Bill—let's call it flexibility—when it came to running in practice, weight training, crap that was inconsequential to me. But the thing I lived and died for was this: *did the Giants win?*

Like I said before, I played to win, I *had* to win. And you win as a *team*.

Come game day I was a wild man, totally intent on willing the team to a win. If there was a big hit I could make, I'd do it. If it was getting into the heads of the other guys, lighting a fire under their behinds, I'd do that. I would have gone out there and dragged the whole entire offense across the goal line if the rules allowed it.

On the sidelines, I was always pretty much frothing at the mouth.

"Let's go out there like a *bunch of crazed dogs* and have some *fun!*"

"We gotta get *crazy* out there! You can't play like that. We're *flat,* man, *really flat*—come *on,* we know what this game means!"

I'd be screaming in people's faces if they did anything wrong, pacing back and forth, about to explode.

I was so intense about winning that I pissed more than a few people off. If you wanted me to respect you, you had to want to win as much as I did—or at least be somewhere in the same galaxy. But if I didn't think you were serious about winning, get out of my face. So you can imagine what I was like during our 3-12-1 season.

They'd send me in to ream the guys out at halftime.

"You #@%&ing guys are so *SOFT* out there! This is *embarrassing!* I can't believe you #%$@*#!ing guys are *not performing!*"

I scorched a few dudes. I had zero tolerance for wusses.

Bottom line, strong teams have strong teammates. And I couldn't have done what I did unless I had some of the best. Some of them are Hall of Famers now, some are going to be, most probably won't. But they're all guys who strapped it on every game, year in and year out, and who made me a better player. Who were part of all the greatest things I did. Or who played great on the other side of the ball. Or who coached me, guided me, led me.

The strength of the Giants has always been the defense. And our defense was not a finesse defense. It was a knock-you-on-your-butt defense. Nothin' too fancy about it. We'd just outplay you, outrun you and definitely out hit you. And nobody showed that smash-your-head-in spirit like the Giants' linebacking unit.

If you need to be a little nuts to play football, then you got to be certifiable to play linebacker. From high school through college and the pros, the linebackers I've come across have always been intense and out on the edge. Or over it. Like Jack "Hacksaw" Reynolds, who played for the Rams and 49ers. When he was in college he got so ticked at losing a game that he sawed a car in half. With the Niners, he used to drive to games in full uniform, sitting in his Chevy in traffic with his helmet on. Does that sound completely messed up to you? To me it makes perfect sense. There's just something in the life of the linebacker that makes him a little...*extreme*. He's in on every play, all over the field, rushing the passer, dropping in to coverage *and* stopping the run. He's got the speed of the cornerback's world, but the hitting is a hell of a lot harder. The intensity gets to you after a while, I guess.

During my thirteen years with the Giants, I had the chance to play with a lot of different linebackers, but the one group I really bonded with was Harry Carson, Brad Van Pelt and Brian Kelley. Those guys had been holding down the linebacker corps in the 4-3 before I got there. So they were a tight unit already—tight enough to be the ones griping about the Giants' plans to draft me.

Once Brad and Brian warmed up to me, I found out those two knew how to party. Brad was the true party animal—although at that level of partying, who was keeping score? Brad was a very strange dude with a twisted, dry sense of humor. Off the field he seemed laid back, in a way, but he was a hard-nosed punisher on Sundays.

Brad and Brian were tight. You would usually see them together, holding down the middle on the field, standing on the sidelines or partying hard wherever the scene was. Except that Brian was actually Mr. Responsible. He was also the Brain—one of the smartest dudes I ever played with. He knew that playbook inside and out. More than once he was the one telling the coaches what to do. He was not shy about sharing his knowledge with me, either: when I was a rookie I blew my assignment at a home game, messing up a play, so Mr. Kelley lost it on me with 75,000 fans watching. I just hope the TV cameras didn't pick it up.

It was too bad that Brian and Brad couldn't be there with us when we finally made it to the promised land. When they got traded I felt like the rug had been pulled out from under me. They'd been on losing teams for so long, though, Bill felt like we needed some fresh blood, dudes who didn't *expect* to lose. We did make it to Super Bowls after he got rid of all those people, so maybe he was on to something.

Harry Carson, the left outside linebacker, was a mentor in other ways. Even before I was actually drafted, Harry called me up at Carolina to assure me that everything was going to be cool with me on the team. Then, at my first minicamp, he took me out to dinner. He took some interest in me, wanted to help guide me through life in pro football. That meant a lot, especially with none of the other veterans giving me the time of day. And over the years, Harry continued to look out for me, calm me down and make me work.

I remember one time when we were playing the Redskins, John Riggins, a 230-pound bull of a back, put his knee right into my head. I was not in my right mind. Harry looks over to check on me, like he always did, and sees me just sort of floating around in the middle of the field. "Get lined *up,* LT," he yells. But I don't really know where *up* is. I don't know where *anything* is. So he calls time out and leads me over to the sidelines. That was Harry.

He was a born leader, on and off the field. He was the motivator of the team, the preacher and the dad. Over the years I learned some things about leadership from Harry, too. But I put them into practice in a different way—an LT way. Like making a point about taking responsibility for your assignments by picking up a young defensive back, slamming him against the wall and screaming at him in front of the whole team.

"Our defense was **not** a finesse defense. It was a knock-you-on-your-butt defense."

"We'd just **outplay you,** outrun you and definitely out hit you."

Harry is a complex dude, though. Sometimes he'd overthink stuff—or overtalk it. He'd speechify us to death in team meetings, or carry private team issues over to the press. Harry really took me under his wing, but then pretty soon I took over from him as defensive leader and Big Giant. Later, after he retired, I felt like he was dissing me and the Giants. Things were tense for a few years. So when Harry came to my induction into the Hall of Fame, it really meant a lot to me. I realized that he was my brother—and always had been.

Harry finally joined me in the Hall in 2006, and I'm damn proud to be there with him.

Harry, Brian and Brad only played together for three seasons, but it felt longer than that. On the field we had our own kind of playbook—but it wasn't on paper. What it came down to was that those guys had my back. X's and O's weren't my scene, remember—whoever got the ball, that's where I'm going. So Harry used to say, "LT, do whatever you want to, I'll just back you up." And Brian was always there to make sure I made it to practice on time. Brad, he always bought the beverages. You could depend on those guys.

After practice, we just gravitated together, and the only question was what club we were going to. Whatever we did, we just had a damn good time.

People still call us "the Crunch Bunch." We've remained good friends over the years, talking regularly, hanging out, vacationing together sometimes and appearing at charity events. Brian is a financial advisor now and handles some of my money. I figure if he could tell me what play I should be running he can tell me what to do with my finances. Those guys have still got my back!

Of course I was lucky to have Harry on the other side of the field for six more years. And I've been able to play with some other great linebackers in later years, guys like Carl Banks. Ugly mother, but the best run-stuffer I ever saw. You want to run a play away from me? Fine. Meet Mr. Banks—happy now? Carl was another leader—the team elected him co-captain with me and Phil Simms—but more of a leader-by-example type. I also got to play with Gary Reasons, and later Steve DeOssie and Pepper Johnson, all-Pro-caliber guys who I went to Super Bowls with. Steve was a little bit in the Brad mold: a wild, Harley-riding party dude with a left-field sense of humor. Steve and I used to look out for each other as we copped Z's on the floor during team meetings. Pepper was a great guy and still is a good friend—full of *up* energy. A fine LB, too—we had a rock-hard crew with him anchoring the unit on the other side.

But without the studs the Giants had up front, we linebackers would basically have been roadkill. Leonard Marshall was a very serious, 285-pound dude who hit like he was in the demolition business. I loved doing stunts with Leonard that would get one of us past the blockers and on top of the quarterback. My favorite Marshall moment was when he knocked Joe Montana out of the game in the 1990 NFC Championship game with a wicked helmet shot to the back. Now *that* is my kind of football.

Jim Burt, our nose tackle, was another guy I had a complex relationship with. Maybe we're too much alike. In-fricking-tense, in other words. We'd get into it, tee off on each other in the locker room, in the middle of a game, on the damn golf course. But you know what? Everybody's got a role to play. If Jimmy and I could bring that out in each other, great. I won two championships lined up behind that dude, an absolute baller who could control a line like you never saw.

And George Martin, the other defensive end. Yet another tough dog who could put the fear of God into the offense. George has been an interesting cat to have in my life...most of the characters in the LT story are wild men who rocked the party, the Streaters and Van Pelts and DeOssies, but George is a Christian man. When the rest of us were figuring out where we were going to misspend our youths after practice, George would sit there reading scripture. I respected that, though, and I listened to the man as much as my itching insides would let me. He walked the walk, too: George came to Linda's aid and did a lot of the grunt work to pull me through the toughest times in my life. It was totally on the down-low; just a quiet word from Parcells was all he needed. And as I went through deeper and deeper valleys, George was there to help me and Linda out, showing me the tough love and not letting go.

working folk, which a lot of us happened to be. What I learned was that Phil grew up in the Kentucky countryside without much more than the basics—a lot like me, in other words.

And I think his performance in Super Bowl XXI against the Broncos was one for the ages. He definitely reached down deep for that game—that whole season, in fact.

Talking about Simms I can't forget Jeff Hostetler. He lived up to his nickname and was a true "Hoss" subbing for Simms in the '90 season—guiding us to our second Super Bowl. Hoss was an intense competitor, and the biggest competition he had was with Phil and the other quarterbacks for the job, and with the rest of us for respect.

There are a couple more guys I have to talk about or this won't be complete. Bill Parcells and Bill Belichick.

First, Belichick. Bill Belichick was my first linebackers coach, and then defensive coordinator under Parcells. I'm going to be my usual candid self and say that I was not crazy about the guy. He had his problems with me too. Call it a clash of styles. Any kind of crap you could think of to obsess on, he was all over it, jamming me up and busting my chops. Bill Bedcheck, we called him.

It usually came down to the meetings. Now, I went 100% in games and 100% on my social agenda, so I had to have some downtime, you know what I'm saying? And meetings, hey, they're quiet, chairs are comfy, lights are low during films…they're a good place to recharge. Once, before our first Super Bowl, we were going over some scouting report as thick as the phone book. I was sitting up, my papers in reading position, propped on my elbows with the look of a dude who is totally wrapped up in what he's reading. Belichick made some point about it, said, "Got that, LT?"

No response.

"Got that, LT? Hey...LT?"

He came over and shook me. That must have been when my dark glasses fell off.

I was out like a light, snoring,

"This," he said, looking real serious at everyone else, "is not to be tolerated."

Over the years I forced him to come up with all kinds of responses to that particular situation.

But like I said to him on another occasion when he woke me up, "You either get me on Thursday or you get me on Sunday." My three hours on game day were worth 50 hours of anybody else's meetings. There was a lot of crap I didn't do, from running laps to weight lifting. It didn't fit into my game plan—didn't directly help me to put the QB on the ground on Sunday. And when it came to Belichick's kind of obsessive game prep, sure, some people needed to have it. But with me, well...when the rubber hit the road, when the ball was snapped, I knew just what needed to happen.

Belichick could never completely get that, though. So being me, I couldn't help but jive him. He'd go through this game plan presentation— every down, every quarter, the other team's passing tendencies, running tendencies, the whole nine yards. Then as we were coming off the field from our warm-up, I'd ask him when the other team liked to pass and run—like I hadn't heard a goddamn word. He was all too ready to believe it.

It was so easy to mess with him. The reality, though, is that Bill Belichick is one brilliant, strategic guy. His defensive game plans were works of art, I got to say. He's got his X's and O's down to a level few will ever come close to. It's no surprise that he's been winning Super Bowls in New England. I'm sure he's not done yet, either. You want to know his real brilliance, though? Leaving holes in his schemes big enough for LT. I know that wasn't easy for him—it definitely stretched his mind—but then there wasn't a lot about me that was easy for Belichick to take.

Parcells, he didn't care about the details like Belichick. He just wanted you to go out, shove it down the other guys' throats and win.

When Bill took over in '83, a lot of guys didn't respond to him. He had a rep as a disciplinarian. Yes, he will call you on the carpet—he figures if you can't take him, you can't take the pressure when the game's on the line.

Bill Parcells is not a coach for wusses.

He would razz guys, needle them, drive them frigging crazy. Me, Simms, Hoss, anybody. We all blew up at him eventually. But Bill is the only coach I ever met who could have got me to perform at the level I did for as long as I did.

And it's worth saying that I gave him the chance. I kept the Giants from firing his big butt.

The '83 was such a messed-up season that George Young and the rest of the Giants management had decided Parcells just wasn't going to work out. Or at least that he was expendable enough to take the blame for it. They were about to can him and pick up Howard Schnellenberger from the U. of Miami. After three years, though, the connection between Bill and myself was already strong enough for me to know I didn't want to play for anyone else. So when my agents had the Giants buy my contract back from Trump at the end of the season, there was this last little condition I wanted before I put my "LT" on the dotted line…

So Bill stayed. And LT was happy. And the Giants, give or take three years, got a Super Bowl, and eventually another one.

That was just one link on a whole chain of connections tying me and Bill together. I got to admit, we were close. We would talk all the time. Some weird father-son business going on there. That didn't mean he wasn't

the most *in-your-face* dude I ever met. I guess the more he liked you, the better you were, the more he rode you. But I got him back whenever I could. I still get off on the time I locked him out of practice.

He said we were practicing like crap and walked off the field with his assistants. "Coach yourselves," he said. "I'm not wasting my coaches' time." So I locked the gate after him. I ran the practice myself, me and Phil Simms. Eventually he came back with his guys and yelled at me to frigging let him in, but I wouldn't. We were having a great practice.

We won the game that week. And now that I think about it, I don't think I would have been into that practice if he hadn't told us we weren't worth coaching.

Like I said, Bill got me. He *knew* that he got me, too—and he used that to the hilt. Bill may not be the X's and O's guy that a Bill Belichik or Bill Walsh is. He's a great motivator, yeah—but he's not the best there, either. Bill is a master *manipulator*. Like the practice story I just mentioned. Who was pulling whose strings on that one?? Bill knows the tools he's got in his box, and he knows just how to use them. It's probably not the first thing people think of when they talk about the Big Tuna, but I think he's one of the best psychologists in football.

I've told you the one thing fires me up to do something is to tell me it can't be done. Well, as my career went on, Bill would tell me before just about every game against Washington that the Redskins didn't think I could play anymore. I must have heard that crap fifty times. And it always worked.

Bill could see from the first preseason that I was a guy who lived life in the fast lane. When the partying and other stuff surfaced, he wasn't surprised one bit. To him, it was just like skipping the weights, and the running, and copping my Z's in meetings. It came with the package. That was me as much as winning games for him on Sunday was. And you either threw the package out, or used what you had. So as long as I was bringing it on game day, he gave me the space I needed to be LT.

"When you can do what I do on the field, maybe you can get out of running in practice, too," was what I said.

Did I get preferential treatment? Yeah.

Some players said it wasn't fair.

"I'm not interested in being fair," Bill said. "I'm interested in being right."

And being right, in Bill's book—and mine—means winning.

CHAPTER 06 | Talking About A Revolution

How I Changed the Game—Brought to You by the Big Tuna

I didn't plan on changing the game. I just wanted to play it.

But look at the game after LT.

The standard two backs in the backfield became one back. That was Joe Gibbs trying to free up more blockers to save his QBs. And the more teams I played, and the more other guys were rushing from the outside linebacker position, the more it spread.

Offensive line formations shifted. You have guards and other interior linemen available to handle rushing LBs and other weird things defensive coordinators cooked up out of the 4-3.

Defenses changed, too.

I definitely changed the linebacker position, or at least the way coaches could think about it. Before, linebackers were more passive. They'd stop the run when it came through or dropped back into pass protection. Suddenly here I was, speed-rushing the QB, bringing it hard from the outside. So some people say I created a whole new position, the "rush linebacker" or just the "Lawrence Taylor position."

There were guys who came along after me like Charles Haley, pass rushers who had what looked like similar assignments and similar freedom to go where the action was. Great players, no doubt—you did *not* want Charles Haley in your face. Thing is, and I don't want to sound arrogant, but the "revolution" I started was not about the position. It wasn't about the responsibilities I had, either. It was about the kind of athlete I was. The whole enchilada—speed, vision, physicality, judgment—that let me dictate games the way I did. One guy who—just because he was there— was going to spin the other coach's entire damn offensive game plan.

You see a few of those in the league these days. They're not necessarily linebackers, either—I like that kid Troy Polamalu in Pittsburgh, for instance, the safety with all the hair. He's one guy I'll turn on the TV to watch. I like the way he controls the whole game, a lot like I used to do from my spot.

After LT, a lot of things were different in the NFL. But then I played at a different level. I played a different type of game. You want me to break it down for you, here's some of what I brought to it.

Speed. I ran a 4.5-second 40. A lot of receivers would be happy with that speed. Well, I'm no DB, but I was fast enough to get into the backfield before anyone expected to see me there. That's why a lot of the time I was pulling quarterbacks down from behind—or catching running backs who hadn't left the backfield. It also gave the side-to-side speed I needed to shut down plays they were trying to run away from me. This was what I had, though: *closing speed*. Seeing my man, going after him and shutting him down. Nobody ever put a stopwatch on "closing speed." But I'll tell you this: put a ballcarrier in front of me and I was *way* faster than 4.5.

Behind the speed, though, there was *technique*. For example, I had to learn the right angles in order to reach quick backs on the other side of the field. And what I found is that collaring a runner from behind is actually *faster* than trying to get set up in front of him. In front of the line of scrimmage, you've got all these linemen beating on each other. Go behind the line and the only thing in your way is some pissant QB. And let's just say I didn't have Ron Jaworski throwing too many body blocks for Wilbert Montgomery.

Strength. Harder to put numbers on this one. I was never much for weights. But put 300 pounds of Joe Jacoby between me and Joe Theismann and I'd throw him down like a sack of potatoes.

Vision. I would see the whole field at once, up and down the line, from the center back to the halfback in an "I" formation, all of it scrunched down into one neat little movie, everything going in slow-mo. Which way is the line moving? Where's the ball? Where are the holes? All of it right in front of me, *whap*, just like Madden with his Telestrator.

But in addition to the big picture, you've got to see the little things.

I've played a lot of cards. Spent thousands of hours looking for tips about the other dude's hand. One reason I could never be a systems guy is because the information I needed most was in the "tells." Every team had 'em. Maybe it was the twist of the neck. The eyes. The stance. Pressure

on the fingertips. Where the foot was pointing. Is the weight forward (run) or back (pass)?

A lot of the vision thing is about memory. Like I said, I must have had hundreds, thousands of "tells" stored up there—sets I'd seen, moves I'd seen, plays I'd seen. I knew that Joe Montana looked straight down at his center's back right before the snap. With the speed rush, those little things that told me when to go were how I got an edge.

People said I had football *instinct,* or maybe that I played by sense of smell. Hey, I was just *thinking* faster than anyone else. I'd process a thousand pieces of information in a split second. Like a supercomputer. Could I explain that process to you, everything that went into it? Hell, no. Too much data, way too fast. But I could explain the result: I knew what to do. You want to call that instinct, go ahead.

Here's what else I was about:

Playing Through Pain. I had a boatload of pain, and I felt every bit. Sometimes I had pain so bad there were tears coming out of my eyes. What else I had, though, was tolerance for it. I could probably play with as much pain as any other guy in the league.

Playing in pain is like forcing yourself to play when you're tired. It's just a matter of tricking yourself. Because I could do that, I could strap it on and win games even when my body was messed up. I was out because of injuries two and a half games in my pro career. A lot of other games, maybe I should have been out. I played New Orleans in 1988 with a wrecked shoulder I had to keep sticking back in its harness. But it wasn't even a question. We had other guys hurt worse. And we had to win. *I* had to win. End of story.

What Bill Parcells said about it was, "His will made him ignore things like pain. People call it determination…whatever it is, he just had it. He just did not give in. He was going to make it the way he wanted to make it."

Yeah, you could say that. I guess my need to win was a lot higher than my need to avoid pain.

But I also had this ability to recover from injury faster than other people. (I don't know if I still do...it's hard to fracture your tibia playing golf.) One of our team doctors, Allan Levy, said, "Lawrence doesn't heal like normal people do. Either he can heal much faster or he can function with a lot more damage than most people can." Ray Handley, our offensive coordinator and then coach in '91 and '92, said I was a "medical marvel."

Because I knew I could take the pain, and heal up faster than anyone else, I didn't think twice about anything. And that meant I was coming at you full speed every time whether you were John Riggins or Walter Payton or some big mother of a tackle. Just like when I was a kid jumping out of trees or tackling cops, avoiding pain was never near as important as the rush that contact gave me. That's what scratched the itch. So that's why I didn't have any fear.

Offensive Defense. To me, if you play a "read and react" style of defense, you've already lost the game. That's why I was not really into the game as much my last couple of years under Rod Rust, Coach Ray Handley's defensive coordinator. My defensive philosophy was to play defense *offensively. Dictate it,* in other words. Don't wait for them to bring the game to you, take it to them. Push them back, drop them for a loss, intercept, go for the strip.

And get the damn ball back.

I always looked for something extra in my defensive play. Being a fast, weak-side linebacker, I was usually coming up on the quarterback's blind side—or behind a runner. That put me in a perfect position not only to drop the guy for a loss, but to get the ball away from him. The QB's standing there with his back to you, holding the ball out behind him before he brings it forward for the throw...dag, it's like an apple just waiting to be picked. Wrap the mother up and drop him, yes. But bring the other arm down and knock that ball away. It was almost too easy sometimes.

And the running back—he's looking *upfield* for tacklers and holes. The last thing he's thinking about is 243 pounds of LT dropping down on his backside. Not too hard to get the ball loose if you're in a place he didn't expect you to be.

That's how you force 33 fumbles.

Look around the league—everybody's got the strip move now. Somewhere someone was looking at my highlight tapes. That's LT stuff.

And I don't know how many yards I got the other guys to lose, but I'd bet it's more than the career yardage of some running backs I played against.

But all that is only half the picture.

On any other team, Lawrence Taylor would have been a great linebacker. On the Giants, I became *LT*. And that was because I had Parcells.

Like I said, Parcells knew how to use the tools in his box. And what he saw in me was someone who was playing the game at a different level. Someone he could get the most out of by taking off the leash. It wasn't an immediate thing, but after less than a season of seeing my "mistakes" turn into sacks and fumbles, he got with the program. He started to give me more and more rope, first as defensive coordinator under Perkins and then as head coach. He let me rush the passer, shut down the runner or drop back into coverage depending on what I felt was going to work in that moment. That's not to say I didn't have assignments—Belichick would

"I guess my need to win was a lot higher than my need to avoid pain."

never let someone have *no* assignments. But I had options, a range of things I could do. And the system was designed around that. Guys like Harry Carson, Brian Kelley, Pepper Johnson or Gary Reasons had assignments that backed me up, whatever I did, lest someone break contain on my freelancing.

You have to understand how far out of the box that was. Systems ruled then. You had these systems like the Doomsday Defense in Dallas or the Steel Curtain in Pittsburgh, where great players like Randy White or Mean Joe Greene all had their jobs within the coach's system. If you didn't fit in the system, sorry, you were out. Would LT have fit into a system like that? I could have done it, yeah, and played at the All-Pro level. But I wouldn't have become LT—the dude who made coaches shift their offenses, the force that changed the game.

Don't get the idea that after me every club's system went out the window. Systems still rule. Most people need that structure. They need direction, plays, assignments. With everything going down on defense once the ball is snapped—the speed, the hitting, the people running right at you—most guys need their assignments to keep them from wigging.

Most guys. Not me.

Systems are what drive me crazy. And the bodies flying, the smack of contact, all of it happening at once—I just love that business. That's my office. That's when I'm thinking clearest.

Bill could see that. So he could either give himself gas trying to jam me into the system—or just take me off the leash. And after he did, it was me who ended up dictating the system. Hey, after three or four years I could spew the playbook at you in my sleep. But I could usually come up with something *better* in my sleep, too.

Check it: Lamar Leachman was running game films one morning in 1986, telling us about the pass rush schemes for the game. That was when the guys started hearing a noise from the back of the room. Snoring. Everybody turned around to see me, as usual, slumped down in my chair, my hat pulled down low over my dark glasses. I don't know if I'd slept the night before, but if I had, you know it wasn't much.

Lamar had seen my act. He just kept on running the films and talking. But a few minutes later, I woke up, looked up at the screen and saw something I didn't like. I told Lamar to turn the projector off.

"That's all wrong," I said.

I walked up to the whiteboard, took a marker and started diagramming. "Look, right end does this, left end does this, inside rush should be like this..." I scribbled down the formation and told Lamar to copy it into the playbook. Then I sat down and went back to sleep.

Yeah, drop me onto a football field and I'm master of the universe.

Beyond the football field, though, it was a different story.

The Rocky Road To The Big Dance

Kicking Off an MVP Season with Golf Therapy

"The Giants are the Red Sox of football. They will break your heart." That's what the papers were saying before the 1986 season.

You couldn't blame them. In 1984 and 1985 we'd gotten *so* close, losing to the 49ers and the Bears, the eventual Super Bowl winners. But we were getting good, even really good. Phil Simms was healthy and coming into his own. We were starting to add a legit offense to our defense—which was nails, as always.

We were knocking on the door. Maybe this was the year we'd get in.

Arriving in camp, I had more immediate personal goals to think about, though. Like crawling back into pro football and the rest of my life.

I had had some rough times before the season started. My lifestyle off the field had caught up with me. I had to clean myself up. It was tough, real tough, but now I was focused. I had to be.

I surprised everyone by showing up to our Pleasantville training camp early. I knew I was going to have to work at this camp, couldn't be up to my usual bed-check Houdini act. Bill and my teammates had been solid while I was dealing with my stuff, sending me support and shielding me from the press. They wanted me to do well now. On the other hand, they'd be gunning for me if I didn't toe the line. And so would Linda.

I attended meetings and stayed awake. I even lifted weights. And I played a hell of a lot of golf.

Golf is a very big thing in my life. You'd think the game would be a little slow for LT—but then you've never played with me. Every putt is do or die. Just ask my golf buddy, Michael Jordan. I guess there is something about the relative quiet of the game, and the fact that instead of 22 humongous dudes going at top speed, smashing each other's faces in, it's just you and this one little ball. Ever since Ivery taught me to play in college, I've loved golf. Whatever it was about that game that quieted me down, well, that was salvation after rehab, the one anchor in the ocean of bad times I'd gone through. It was my therapy. George Martin and some other serious spiritual types were trying to approach me about getting deeper with my problems. And life eventually gave me some big head slaps to show I needed more than any nine holes could give. At the time, though, I was a believer in golf therapy. If I was gonna do something, I had to do it *my* way, remember?

Back in camp and in preseason I was focused. All I wanted was the chance to win games and knock some helmets around.

I was grateful—grateful that I was still in the game, and grateful particularly to Bill, who was shielding me from a lot of hungry media people sticking their noses in my face.

And I was angry.

I was angry at a lot of stuff: at the media who thought I was this washed-up, messed-up druggie, and even at Linda for pressuring me to be someone different than who I was. Yeah, I know, I should have been grateful to her. But it's not always that simple in relationships.

Maybe I was really angry at myself. I couldn't figure out how to reconcile the wildness that made me great on the field with life off the field. I don't know. What I do know is that I was one ticked-off linebacker.

I knew I could play; I hadn't lost a step. I was gonna play for the doubters. Gonna play to show they were full of it.

And with all the junk gone from my system, I was really frigging jumpy. I was tired of taking it out on Giants linemen and blocking sleds. I wanted to get into a game and stick some quarterbacks into the ground.

I had a sack and a half in our first game, against Dallas, and made some LT-quality plays. So that was cool...but we lost. Along with everyone else, I got tired in that game. It was hot, it was early in the season....and I still didn't feel like myself. I told myself, son, you're gonna have to do better than that.

Then we started winning. Five straight, in fact. It was the best start we'd had since 1970.

We were starting to get a buzz going. But I didn't get another sack for four games. So the jury was still out on LT. I couldn't quiet down the rumors, the speculation, all the crap. And it just made me angrier. I'm playing for my life here, and these sonsabitches are already writing up the LT retirement story.

It wasn't until the sixth game of the season that I got untracked and had the kind of breakout game that I could shove in their faces. Philadelphia and my old friend Ron Jaworski were in town. You know, maybe I should

have had Jaws be my presenter at my Hall of Fame induction. *Man* he was good for my career! Slowest guy in the league by far. If there'd been another 27 Ron Jaworskis in the NFL, I could have played for another 27 years.

Between him and Randall Cunningham, I got four sacks on that day, eleven tackles, two assists and was named NFC Defensive Player of the Week. *That's* what I'm talking about!

The thing that to me was absurd was that they had this running back blocking me for most of the game. Keith Byars—a rookie running back at that. *Hello?* I guess Coach Buddy Ryan hadn't gotten the memo from the rest of the league—you don't send a boy to do a man's job, and you definitely don't send no running back to block LT. On three sacks I jumped over the dude, went around him and finally just knocked Byars into old Jaws. By the fourth quarter, Buddy had mercy on Jaworski and sent in Cunningham instead. Cunningham was at least a moving target!

After a few years of me knocking him on his tush, Jaworski was getting spooked. One play, he looked out at the defense and yelled, *"Where's 56?"* I popped my head up from across the line and shouted back, "Don't worry, homeboy, I'll be right there. Just hold on a second!"

The whole team was firing on all cylinders in that game. We kicked their rear ends all over Giants Stadium, 35-3. My favorite play wasn't even one of mine—it was when Harry Carson caught an offensive touchdown pass from Jeff Rutledge on a fake field goal. How nice was that? Definitely a pretty moment for the D—we sometimes felt we ought to be playing on both sides of the ball anyway.

The next week we lost to Seattle in a game we should have won—*had* won, except for the damn offense giving it away through turnovers. Overall they were doing better, though, and they did have some key injuries. Studs like tight end Mark Bavaro had gone down. They were even getting ready to stick QB Jeff Hostetler in at tight end. So us defensive guys sucked it up and kept our complaints private. If we were going to win, we were going to win as a team. And our next game was against the Redskins, who, along with the Cowboys, were the heavies of the NFC East. The Giants were coming on now, though, and everybody knew it. This game might be a playoff preview, or a passing of the torch, or I don't know what all. It was going to be a big game—you could feel it.

Our offense lit the place up against the Skins, going up 20-6 in the first half on what would eventually be 181 yards rushing from Joe Morris. Where did these guys come from? Little guy, quiet, didn't look like much in the locker room, hadn't done all that much the year before, but damn! He had 181 yards here, 202 yards there...and the rest of the O was not shabby, either—in fact, it was the defense that almost gave it away this time, when we got burned by some pass plays in the second half. We ended up holding on to pull out a 27-20 win. Now we were in a three-way tie with the Skins and the Cowboys for the NFC East lead.

I kicked Washington all over the lot: eight tackles, two assists and three sacks. If people had not noticed me against Philadelphia, they knew I was in the house now. I wasn't crazy about the way the press reported it, though. "Lawrence Taylor played like the All-Pro of old," the newspaper said. What was *that* about? They might as well have written, "Lawence Taylor has come back from the dead." Man, I'd only been doing this stuff every year for, uh, six years...

The really messed-up thing, though, was that I hyperextended my right elbow in that game. That meant I had to do things like tackling George Rogers and stripping the ball from him all with one arm. While I could wrap guys up with my left, I couldn't do my signature move: axing guys with my right. That was my secret to getting them to drop the ball. Or, if I really hit a home run, to get them out of the game. Basically, my arm was messed up for the rest of the season. Which made my stats that much more impressive.

I ended up having 20.5 sacks on the year, to go with 79 tackles and a bunch of fumbles caused. One big reason '86 was such a big year for me statistically is that Bill was rushing me more. I think he saw that with the abuse I was taking, playing the way I played—we're not even talking about the off-field stuff—I was going to last longer if I rushed 75 percent, 80 percent of the time, rather than dropping into coverage more than half the time. I wasn't complaining. Rushing had always been my thing.

Mark Gastineau of the Jets had set the single-season sack record a few years before. And I know I would have broken that bad boy, except no team wanted me to get it against them. The more sacks I got, the closer I got to the record, the more guards, tackles and big-mofo double-teams were in my face. We did get a hell of a lot of sacks as a team that year, though. So having those interior linemen shut me down meant they weren't blocking Leonard Marshall, George Martin, Carl Banks and the rest of the Big Blue Wrecking Crew.

And there was another consolation for not getting the sack record: league MVP. They hadn't given the MVP to a defensive player since Alan Page in 1970—and they haven't given it to one since. You know what that MVP was to me? Really? It was my statement to the media and everybody else who wrote me off. So my greatness is in the past? OK, then what's *this*, chump?

Well...I somehow didn't put that into my acceptance speech.

And now, as time has passed, I got to give it to those journalists. First of all, I realize they're just doing their job, and their job involves finding a story. Something juicy—maybe even a full-on scandal. I just didn't happen to like being the story. But I will say this: without them doubting me, saying I couldn't do it, I might not have made that great of a comeback.

The MVP was sweet. But what I really wanted was one of those big fat rings with all the diamonds and roman numerals on it. And the way things were going, it was starting to look like my boys and I were all going to get one.

After the Redskins game, we won every game the rest of the regular season—including our second game against the Redskins. Beat 'em 24-14, and it wasn't that close. I mean we really messed them *up*. Phil Simms was stepping up his game more and more, mixing up the short dinks with long bombs. The Skins keyed on Joe Morris and he still got 62 yards. I had

three sacks. Along with George and Leonard, I was in Jay Schroeder's face all day, forcing interceptions and generally making his life miserable.

Going into the playoffs we were *ssssmokin'*—we won our last two games by a combined score of 82-31.

But check this: I was starting to see the banners at Giants Stadium. They said, *"LT IS GOD."*

I love the fans. You don't know what it's like to run out there at the start of a game with thousands of people chanting "LT! LT! LT!" Sends chills up my spine to think of it now! You know, though...well, this may sound wack from a guy who danced on a bar top in front of a hundred partyers—but I'm a private guy. Never did too well when the attention got too up close and personal. Like people jamming me up for autographs when I'm out trying to have a good time. Or hanging signs saying that I'm God, or wanting to tell me their life stories or trying to latch on to me in some weird way. I've gotten better with the autographs, but when people start with the personal stuff, I always say, "Hey, anything but the story."

I played great for the Giants, I helped get 'em two championships, and I think people in New York and New Jersey mostly like the way I strapped it on, left it all on the field. The way I sacrificed my body and played hurt. Some guys from that area feel this intense connection with me. OK, that's cool...as long as they don't get too close, you know what I'm saying?

I was just a blue-collar kind of player on a blue-collar team. And a guy who did a lot of stupid stuff during his time, too.

I ain't nobody's god.

I had always cared most about our team winning, was very passionate about that. But I used to feel like I could carry the whole thing myself. And like I had to, when the offense was backfiring. Now Phil Simms, Mark Bavaro, Joe Morris and all those guys were playing championship football.

I'd also been humbled a little bit. I knew I was lucky to still be playing. And getting double- and triple-teamed I was playing a different role. Keeping the O-line busy so someone else could have a star turn. A Leonard Marshall or a George Martin or a Jim Burt.

We kept on going into the playoffs. The 49ers came in for the first round—Jim Burt knocked Joe Montana out of the game with a concussion, I ran an INT back thirty-four yards for a TD and we schooled those guys, 49-3. Frisco had kicked us back down the stairs so many times in the postseason, so it felt real good. (I'm not saying we ran up the score, but...)

Could it get better? Check this: NFC Championship game playing the Redskins for the third time that year, at home. I was double-teamed, triple-teamed, quadruple-teamed again, and I got hurt in the third quarter and had to come out. But my boys were more than happy to fill in and we *spanked* the Skins, 17-0.

Hey, now! We had won eleven straight games, outscored the other guys in the playoffs, 66-3. California here we come—we were going to the Show. Super Bowl XXI.

I was real quiet as the Redskins game ended, sitting there on the sideline with my ski mask on in that cold, hard wind while all the red, white and blue confetti came down from the stands and whipped around over the field. I was happy, man, deeply happy. This was what I'd worked for. But I was also reflective. I know, not your usual LT thing, but hey. It had been a long journey. Just that year alone.

I had almost slipped over the edge, been dragged back by my wife, gone through rehab, driven around the US several times, played about seven thousand holes of golf—and helped take my team to the Super Bowl. I'd set out a goal of playing myself back into the elite of my sport, and of sticking it to the doubters and haters. And I'd exceeded anyone's expectations doing it. If someone had scripted this bad boy, Hollywood would have turned it down. It just wasn't believable.

I guess I was having a hard time believing it myself.

Well, it got even weirder once we arrived in Pasadena to play the Denver Broncos. There were just so many cocked-up media events, stupid questions and people trying to cash in on the event with any kind of crap they could think of. Of course, I was happy to do my part and pump the hype up even more:

"I can be an @#$!%. Nasty, lousy, mean people are the guys who get the farthest... I love the contact. It makes the game real enjoyable. I can't go two or three games without a kill shot. That's when the snot comes from [a quarterback's] nose and he starts quivering on the ground. You want to run the film again and again."

You *got* to love that.

Here's another:

REPORTER: *LT, when are you going to know you're ready?*

LT: *When you feel like slapping your momma.*

Way to run the smack, LT!

REPORTER:
"LT, when are you going to know you're ready?"

LT:
"When you feel like slapping your momma."

My main concern in the week leading up to the Super Bowl was to make sure *I* didn't get slapped. Bill had warned us that "six of you guys are going to be followed by NFL security." You didn't have to be Bill Belichick to figure out one person who was definitely on that list. And guess who nobody wanted to ride with that week?

I managed to keep my nose out of any serious trouble and make it to game day. And *man*, there was some football to play! I was getting pumped. You know me, I'm shaking and cussing and spitting when we're going out against the frigging St. Louis Cardinals—sheeoot, now—here I was at the Big Dance! Getting the guys going, starting some shoving matches. Anything I could do to get the guys riled up, keyed up, jacked up enough to go out there and kick the Broncos in the teeth on Sunday, I was going to do it. And if it meant butting heads, then I was gonna start some fights.

Finally, it was game day. You never saw anything like this spectacle. Music, dancing, hype. A lot of energy in the place. I'm doing my thing on the sideline, crawling out of my skin—let me at 'em!

Finally, the kickoff. Denver came out of the box fast and hard with a razzle-dazzle game that was messing us up. Elway had some legs on him, and was doing some damage, along with trick plays that we weren't expecting to see. We eventually settled down. We had some good defensive stands, I caught Elway for a sack and then George Martin nailed him in the end zone for a safety. The offense had done its part, very decent play, but we still felt flat at halftime—and we were losing, 10-9.

During the halftime break we were quiet. Too quiet. Bill was so ticked off he wouldn't talk to us. So I stepped up. "Listen, guys," I said, "we didn't play no type of football. The score is 10-9, and they got every break,

and we played no Giant football whatso*ever*, not one iota of Giant football. We're about to go out and kick those dogs straight in the tail!"

That pumped 'em up. And then we went out there and shut 'em down.

In the second half the D was nails, closing off the running game, harassing Elway and limiting them to 10 points. On offense, Phil didn't throw one incompletion in the second half. The dude was *All-Universe*, as close to perfect as anyone has ever been in the Super Bowl. He earned that MVP a few times over.

In the end, we'd won 39-20. The Giants were champions of the world. I was happy for my boys. We won as a team, offense and defense both bringing it for sixty minutes.

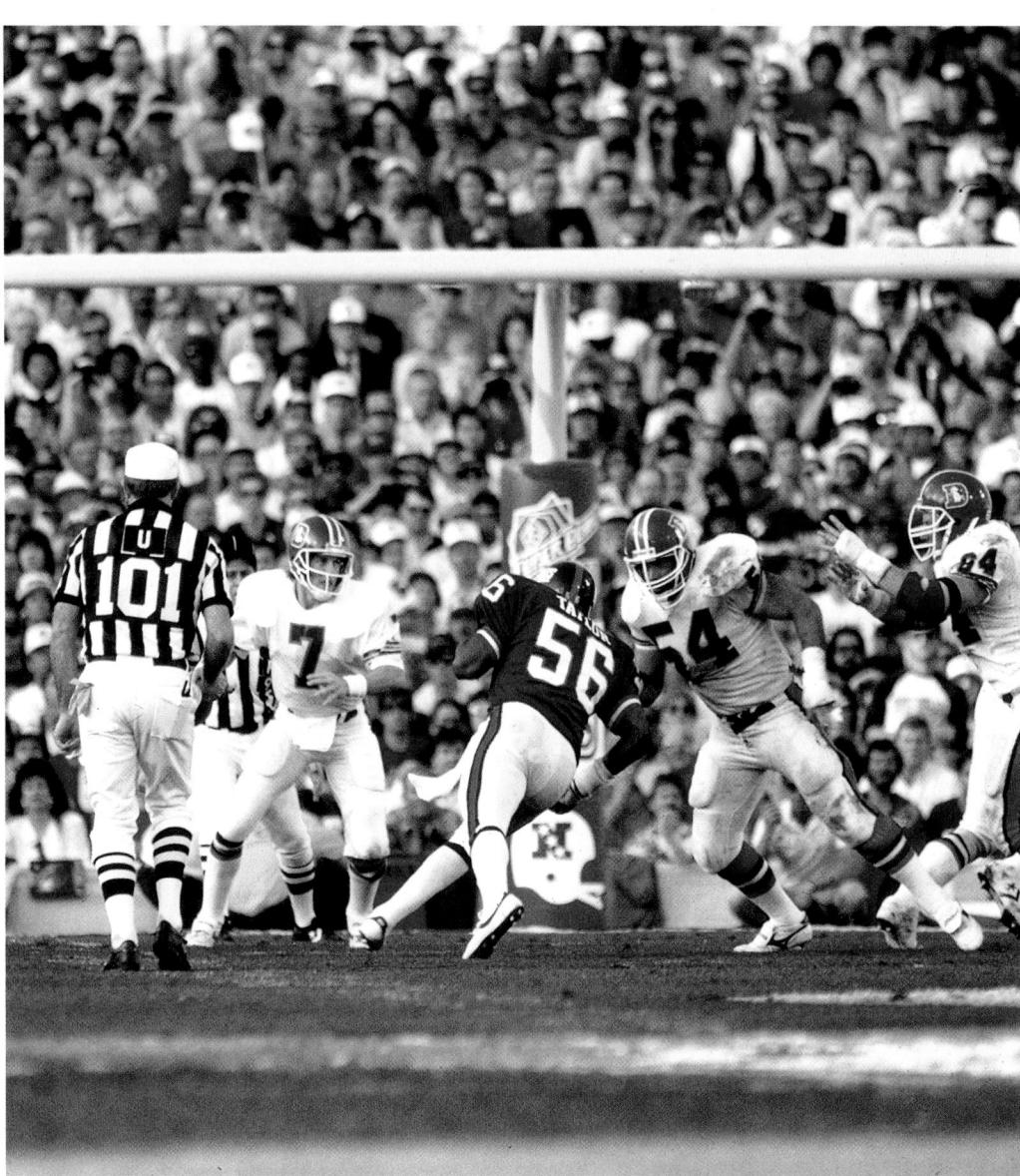

As the game clock counted down, Harry Carson snuck over to the Gatorade bucket and moved in behind Bill. Next thing you know—*sploosh*—the bucket got dumped all over Bill. Harry and the Giants started that tradition. Bill had a little twist on it that evening, though: he whipped out a water gun and spritzed back at Harry. It was time to party. We were like a bunch of kids in the highlight of our football lives. The thrill of victory!

As if winning the Super Bowl wasn't enough, I'd almost broken the sack record, and had made All-Pro and the Pro Bowl and been selected League MVP. It was like the single greatest season anyone has ever had, at least any defensive guy. It was everything I'd worked for, the brass ring, the top of the game...and I was happy...but also tired. Tired and...empty.

All the work, the scrapping, the sacrifice, every bit of my soul that went into that year...it was all over. We had our championship, good. But now that we had our trophy, we were done with the chase. Turned out it was going to be a while before we were going to be chasing after another one.

The run up to the Super Bowl had been an unbelievable buzz, an intense rush that was perfect for an intense player like me. And when the chase was over, I started to feel a need to find that buzz again. Anywhere I could.

CHAPTER 08 | # Playing LT Tough

Getting Double-Teamed by Life

I've always been on a roller-coaster ride, moving too fast to spend time anywhere between high and low. And over the next few years, the climbs on the roller coaster were going to get steeper—and the downhills were gonna get a lot faster.

Like going from 1986 and a championship into a completely messed-up 1987 season. That was another wild ride for me—and the Giants. My NFL roller coaster had just gotten to the top with the Super Bowl win. We all had a nice moment there looking at the view. But man, we came down fast.

Now, the thing about winning the Super Bowl is that the next year you got to live up to it. When you're World Champions, every other team is gunning for you, bringing its "A" game, seeing if it can take you down. Even the NFL office does that, I think. They mess with their schedule, see what they can throw at you. Our first game of the season we played the Bears. That was about as hyped up as you can get with the first game of the season: the past two Super Bowl winners duking it out for bragging rights. Chicago's Super Bowl team showed up, but it seemed like our guys had taken a wrong turn when they left Pasadena. We were dragging on defense, and the Bears' defense and special teams made our offense like it was still in training camp. They handed our rear ends to us on a plate, 34-19.

The next week was no better—we opened at home but gave it up to the Cowboys. As the game wound down I was already a little shaky—I'd gotten rung up good and came out of the game with a concussion.

Of course I went back in. I could walk, after all.

That wasn't the first concussion I'd had, and it sure as hell wouldn't be the last—one time I got dinged really bad and they had to hide my helmet on the sideline so I couldn't go back in. I tell you—no matter what was going on with me, no matter how bad I was hurt, no matter how much I'd been partying, no matter what else was happening in my life, after kickoff there was only one thing that mattered in the world: getting into the game and banging heads.

At the end of the game we had a shot—with six seconds left, 16-14, Raul Allegre lined up 46 yards out for a field goal. Hey, dude had made them from farther than that. You could see him saying that Spanish prayer he always did. Solid kick…but the dog hooked left at the end. Three feet wide. *Daaamn!* It was one of those little things that would have gone right in '86, but didn't in '87.

Well, fact was, we might as well have ended the season right there. The next week all the players in the NFL walked off the job.

Before the season got going, the players and owners had been going at it about player salaries and benefits and free agency and Astroturf and a bunch of different crap. We all hoped Gene Upshaw and our other guys could work it out with the owners, but both sides were pulling more and more crap and finally, bingo, a strike. So guys like Harry Carson were actually walking around outside Giants Stadium with strike signs, which I thought was funnier than anything.

Hey, don't get me wrong, I was all for guys making as much as they could get from the owners. Particularly the fringe players, the special teams guys, third-stringers, etc. It's a brutal, violent profession. Careers are short, and oftentimes they end ugly. So you got to get what you can.

The owners had said OK, you guys do what you want, we're going on with the season. They brought in replacement players, random dudes who hadn't made the teams or hadn't even been drafted.

A couple of weeks go by with these fantasy camp players continuing to lose games for us. I'm sitting around at home, feeling nastier and nastier. And I'm feeling that itch start to eat me up inside. Knowing I'm probably going to get into a very ugly situation unless I do something about it. Like play football.

Like I said, I got only respect and love for most of the guys around the league. But I had no contract problems myself—I was the highest-paid dog on the team. My situation was also a little bit different, because the Giants had covered me big time with all my off-field problems. I felt like I had a debt to Bill and to Wellington Mara, the Giants owner. Mr. Mara was a stand-up person. A really fine man. He'd stood by me, paid me great, believed in me, protected me. So he was one of those people, like my mom, that I could not let down. (Mr. Mara died this past season and, along with a lot of other old Giants, I'll miss him.)

Some of my teammates understood that, I think, and even that I needed to start playing before I started to screw up my life again. Still, other guys were ticked off that I had crossed the picket line.

This was the bottom line for LT, though: LT did what he wanted.

So I called Parcells and told him I was coming back for the game against Buffalo.

I didn't take it all that seriously, just thought it'd be fun, something to do. It ended up being one messed-up game, though. It was like a junior football clinic or something in a playground. Hell, I'd been in more professional games during lunch period in high school. The whole offensive line was holding me like they were going to turn my frigging jersey inside out. The Bills got penalized 7 times for holding me. Hey, they got off easy. It was more like 21 times.

This one guy, Rick Schulte, was in on at least sixteen of those. On one play he even shoved his knee through my face mask as he was getting up off me. Pretty near broke my nose. And then he'd hit me—not clock me, but put enough into it to make me take a serious swing at him. Which, of course, I did. And got a penalty, just like I was supposed to. So on another play I just ran over him, and as he was going down I threw a fist into his throat and rubbed it in there hard. I got my grill real close to him and growled, "How do you like *THAT*, you #@%$?!"

When the game ended I walked up to Schulte, my face ugly. He tensed up, squared for another fight. I could see his fists balling up.

"Hey, you cheap &!@#," I said. "Good game." Then I smiled.

"Th-th-thanks," he said. "It was an honor to play against you."

Hey, these guys were just trying to do a job, doing what the coaches were telling them to do, getting their fifteen minutes of semi-fame.

One thing that was memorable about that game—one of the high points of the season, actually, or would have been if I'd caught it—was the first offensive pass play ever thrown to me in the pros. Jeff Rutledge was the Giants' "regular" second-string QB, a real strong player who had crossed the picket line with me. During the week we'd practiced the play where I'd line up at tight end—my old offensive spot—and Jeff would throw to me. We ran the play late in the game and I got wide open—but Jeff got rushed by the Bills and threw it too high. I leaped up high, got a hand on the sonuvadog—but it bounced away. *Damn!* And there was nothing but open field in front of me. A TD for sure...

So with my own shot at offensive fame down the tubes, we lost, 6-3—and our season was about to go right with it.

The regular guys came back next week—Harry Carson, Phil Simms, Jim Burt and the rest. There was some tension because I'd broken the picket, but it would just have to be there—we had a job to do. We were 0-and-frigging-5. A deep pit, I'm telling you. And unless we won basically every game from there on, that was it.

We didn't win every game. In fact, we lost a lot of them, and finished the season 6-9. Last damn place. First to worst.

And in August 1988 I heard on the radio that I'd been suspended for off-field stuff.

I turned around, drove home, locked myself in my room at home and started crying like a damn baby.

The roller coaster was dropping straight down.

I knew a lot of people had put their butts on the line for me. I'd let them all down. My career was over, my life was over, I couldn't do a damn thing for myself.

That suspension was four of the longest weeks in my entire life. And the media made it feel like eight. It was like throwing raw meat to the lions. Camera crews camped outside the house.

The one thing I knew was that I had to toe the line. I had to stay clean. I had two strikes on me. Another dirty test and I was out of football. That simple.

Meanwhile, back on the field, the Giants were struggling. To fill in for me they'd moved Carl Banks over to my spot on the weak side and switched Pepper Johnson to right inside LB, but it was just throwing everything out of sync. They managed to win two games out of the four I missed, but that was only because of specific mess-ups on the other side of the ball. The D was still getting its posterior kicked. Watching the guys on TV was killing me. I wanted to crawl into the tube and get on the field!

Finally, though, I got back. I was clean and sober again, focused and serious.

Not a good combination…if you were the Washington Redskins.

I wasn't exactly on a rampage, but I was in quarterback Mark Rypien's face by the third play of the game. I broke through the line, put my shoulder down, wrapped him up and axed him with my right arm—*wham*. The combo did what it was supposed to do. The ball came loose, we recovered and one play later we got on the board. I got another sack later, but the main thing is the Giants D was back. What I mean is, when we were doing our thing we were a *machine*. And you take a key part out of any machine, it's not going to work right until you put it back in. I shook the guys up before we went out there, reminded them of who we were and what we were going to do to those chumps. And we did it, beating them 24-23.

I did my part, and it was good to be back out there. But the reality was that suspension had been a sucker punch I hadn't recovered from. Yeah, I'd played OK against DC, but I felt like the fire wasn't really there. I told Bill maybe it was time for me to get out of football. Or at least start fresh on some other team. Bill said I should just suck it up and strap it on for the rest of the season. With me just coming off the suspension, he said the Giants wouldn't get much in return if they tried to trade me.

Bill Parcells, master manipulator. Always knew what to say to a guy. He knew I would go off on something like that. And I did. I was burning up and I started playing like it.

Over the next five games I teed off on QBs, getting eight sacks and 28 tackles. I was just trying to block out all the crap, concentrate on playing like LT.

We were winning, too. Always a picker-upper. The defense was playing great right along with me—everybody swarming in the backfield, jumping on loose balls, just like the old days.

Things were starting to come together. Physically, though, I was starting to come apart.

The injuries were beginning to add up. The season before I had injured my hamstring against Philly, catching Randall Cunningham, and it had never really healed. Against Dallas my two sacks yielded two fumbles, two scores and one torn deltoid muscle. It was up between the chest and the shoulder, and when I raised my right arm—my battle axe—sonofa-*unhhh,* it hurt. I played the next week against the Cardinals and didn't—couldn't—do much. You can't rush with one hand, son.

Squeezed out a sack and a half the next week against Philly and got jammed in the ribs for my trouble. I had a whole mess of pain going into New Orleans. I wasn't the only one hurting, though. Phil Simms had gotten knocked out of the game when Reggie White body-slammed him onto his throwing shoulder, and he wasn't going to be suiting up. Our tight end, Zeke Mowatt, was having a hard time breathing after he got a knee to the chest. On the D, Harry Carson had gone under the 'scope and was out, Carl Banks was sidelined with a bad neck and shoulder, Gary Reasons's shoulder was day-to-day and our stud cornerback Mark Collins had a bad groin pull.

Just another week in the NFL.

I could feel my delt tearing more and more, almost with every play. Couldn't even get my damn shirt on during the week before the New Orleans game. But what was I gonna do? We were in a three-way tie with the Eagles and the Cardinals in the NFC East and needed that game to get a playoff spot. Phil was out, Carl was out, and we *had* to have that game. I had to strap it on. Literally.

The trainers fitted me with this shoulder harness to stabilize the shoulder and minimize the tearing. Somebody pulled a #56 jersey over my head, and I followed Jim Burt through the tunnel into the Superdome.

"This was the bottom line for LT, though...

LT did what he wanted."

And they did: we ended up winning 13-12.

Afterwards there was a moment with Bill where he just put his forehead against mine and looked straight into my eyes. He told me, "You were great tonight." Bill is not exactly your warm and fuzzy kind of guy. So that was, for a couple of tough SOBs, probably the most emotional exchange we ever had. I'd just frigging killed myself to win that game, and he knew it.

I dried my eyes when I faced the press, though. I was loosening up, making nice with them. They asked me what specific parts of the game my torn muscle affected: I grabbed an imaginary golf club and said, "My backswing."

We kept our season alive by playing tough. The next week we beat Phoenix, the week after that we beat Kansas City. It was down to one can't-lose game against the Jets. And with 37 seconds left we had a decent chance, lined up in our goal line defense on our own 5-yard line on third down. They had to get a TD to win. And Ken O'Brien audibled and floated the ball to Al Toon in the end zone. End of game, end of season.

This game…it's all about pain. Take a look back at 1988. For me, there was humiliation—I got suspended and spent the first four weeks of the season in rehab. There was a boatload of physical pain. And then there's that special football pain of losing: of laying it all on the line and seeing it all wash away at the last moment.

It had been one monster of a ride on the coaster these last two years.

Now, if you look at it one way, roller coasters always end up at the bottom.

On the other hand, they always go right back to the top.

CHAPTER 09 The Last Hurrah

'89...'90...XXV

When I first got to the NFL, my life was like those kamikaze plays I ran in training camp. I hurled myself at everything without giving a crap what happened to me. Nine years later, I was not exactly a shrinking violet—I was still gonna mess you up every play—but I'd started to figure out some basic stuff about who I was, what I could do and what I couldn't.

The roller-coaster thing was wearing me down. I had to find some way to do my thing—work hard, play hard—without killing myself or losing my job.

I had a balancing act to do. It wasn't one I was going to really master for years. The roller-coaster ride wouldn't be over for a while. But at least I was starting, and doing what I had to do to stay in the game.

And like it or not, I was becoming a leader.

"L.T., as in 'Leadership Thing.'" That's how the *New York Times* put it. Whatever. Harry Carson had been doing the leadership thing pretty well from even before I got to the Giants, stepping up and making those Hollywood speeches to rally the guys. He was the philosophizer and orator type. But he'd retired at the end of the '88 season, and people had voted me, Carl Banks and Phil Simms as co-captains. Phil was a natural choice, and so was Carl. He was intense but also levelheaded, and looked out for the guys. Me, I guess I had already been kind of a leader there because of my style of play, the way I kicked Giant butt to get the intensity I needed to have around me. But now I was going to have to do the coin tosses and stuff. The point being I was really going to have to step up and help motivate in the locker room, get guys to come correct, have more of a grown-up role. Ha! Good luck with that, son.

What I did know was that I was no Harry Carson. Me, I was going to lead by example.

And I wanted to get to the Super Bowl again. Hopefully, guys would follow.

The thing that really hurt about '88 was that we had played some very good, 8-4 football after I got back from my suspension, good enough to take it to anyone in the postseason. But then, *pwfft*. Not even one playoff game. Still, anyone could see we were getting our act together after '87. We were playing well as a team. Some veterans like Harry, George Martin and Jim Burt had left, and younger guys like Pepper Johnson and Erik Howard were stepping up in their place. We were also picking up free agents, like Steve DeOssie, who were making us that much better.

In '89 we won eight out of our first nine, went 12-4 for the season and won the NFC East. It was another season where I made the Pro Bowl and got a lot of sacks—fifteen, my third most ever, pushing them back 114 yards. Not as good as the year before, when I'd rung up 130 1/2 negative yards on the other guys, or my MVP season in '86, when I'd gotten 137 sack yards, but not bad. That's the offensive defense I like. Move those chains backward.

The thing that was impressive about that, when I look at those numbers now, is that it was getting harder and harder to get those sacks. I wrote about how after my rookie year teams were coming up with schemes to neutralize the LT threat. And like other wonky technical football theories, the anti-LT strategies were evolving. Every week coaches were seeing how many big, fat linemen they could throw at me at once, and what kinds of tricky, gadget blocking schemes they could come up with. Like I said, back in '82, '83 that almost made me lose interest in the whole game— but now I was just philosophical about it. I knew more guys on LT meant penetration somewhere else on the line. So I was cool with that. But also, there was kind of a chess match thing going on each play. What kind of junk was the O-line going to pull, and how was LT going to counter? I won often enough—132 1/2 times, to be exact. (That's my *official* NFL sack total, by the way. They started counting sacks after my rookie year. Just as well. In 1981 I had an unfair advantage: no one had ever seen anything like me.)

Still, '89 was not the season it could have been for me. When we played San Francisco in Week 12, their tight end, Wesley Walls, rolled me with a cut block that left me on the ground, screaming bloody murder. I'd fractured my ankle—well, a hairline fracture at the base of the right tibia. Same difference—it still hurt like a mother. I played the next week against Philadelphia, though, mostly just to keep the guys fired up. Probably not

the greatest idea. We ended up losing. And I was never at full strength the rest of the season.

This is my book, so I'm going to take a moment to go off on the Niners. They always had this squeaky-clean image, like they were this real class act, this finesse team who sipped white wine and would never do anything dirty like the Raiders, oh no. Well, I'm here to tell you that no one cut-blocked like the 49ers. Their OL coach, Bobb McKittrick, taught them the nastiest cut-blocks you would ever see. Or in my case, feel. They were a great team, yeah—four Super Bowls in my time—and it was always a challenge playing against guys like John Ayers and, of course, Joe Montana. But they could also be dirty, underhanded sonsabitches.

Anyway, because we had won the eastern conference in '89, we got to play the wild-card Rams at home. They were the *Los Angeles* Rams then, and our tropical 37-degree game-time temp was bound to freeze their Beach Boy butts off. And we played a pretty good game. Still, the football gods are some twisted dudes. We lost, 19-13.

But that's football. Any given Sunday.

Going into 1990, I decided that, hell, I'd been in nine straight Pro Bowls, was making the Giants one of the top teams in the NFC and was the team's biggest draw in the nation's biggest market. I wanted to be compensated for that. Reggie White, the Eagles' defensive end, had signed a contract that was netting him $1.35 million a year for four years. I wanted that kind of money. In fact, I wanted *twice* as much. I mean, come on—we'd been to twice as many playoff games since Reggie had come over from the USFL, not to mention winning a Super Bowl.

The Giants came back with $1.2 million. That wasn't a lot more than what I was getting paid already.

George Young thought he had me by the short and curlies because I'd been suspended and had two strikes on me, and because at thirty-one, I was getting up there. He thought nobody would want me. So I had my agent, Joe Courrege, shop me around. He got George to give him a letter saying the Giants would do a trade. The Eagles were interested and so were the Oilers. Probably a dozen other teams would have been, but that was enough. George Young sat up and took notice.

Ultimately, I thought the Giants would cough. I knew they wanted to keep me, but on the other hand they'd also tried to trade me in '89. They got to look at which side their bread was buttered on. For me, it was easier to keep playing for Bill, keep working with my boys in the Blue. But if it didn't work out, well, I *had* been thinking about starting over again somewhere else. Maybe now was the time to do it. Ultimately, it was a business thing.

Players can get passionate about their teams just like the fans, but they've got usually four or five years to do the best they can for themselves. So if that means bleeding green instead of blue, well, go Eagles.

The Giants had the right of first refusal, and they were dealing with us again. But they were doing it in Giants style, which was to diddle around until the very last minute. In the end, and I do mean the end—four days before our season opener against the Eagles—we worked out a deal that would pay me $7.5 million over three years. It was the biggest deal in history for a defensive player. The previous record holder had been…Reggie White.

I walked into Bill Parcells's daily press briefing right after I signed and basically took over the mike. I was pumped. The media guys wanted to know about the reports that we might work out a trade. I told them I'd always known I wasn't leaving New York.

A reporter asked, "What about the Eagles rumor?"

"I don't like green," I said. "Except for money."

After playing golf all summer, I basically threw on my uniform and lined up against the Eagles. I was sucking on the oxygen, but I sacked Randall Cunningham three times, got seven tackles and forced a fumble. Not bad for an old, out-of-shape guy. I told the reporters afterward that I was going to go home and have Geritol.

I was staying clean.

Not everyone believed it, of course. But it didn't matter to me—I was just gonna be LT.

What I knew was that I played wild and I lived wild. That wildness was like an animal. And if you don't feed an animal, it's not going to be there for you. Maybe most people would be wiped out by my social life, but all that fast-living, fast-driving, hard-partying buzz during the week just charged me up—and I plugged it into every game. Brought a stone maniac energy nobody else could match and came at those dirty dogs like a natural disaster.

I just had to do it smart. Which meant no drugs, but still being LT when it counted—on and off the field.

I don't think the Giants are ever again going to get off to a start like we did in 1990: we won the first ten games. Some were blowouts, some were close, but we kept finding a way to win. The offense was doing its job. Got some nice play from Phil, when he was healthy, and guys like Ottis Anderson, Dave Meggett and Rodney Hampton, who ate up the minutes. But as usual, the team was mainly about the defense.

I stayed healthy—and made the Pro Bowl for the tenth straight time—but it was not the greatest year statistics-wise. In one six-game stretch in the middle of the season Carl Banks was out, so I had to play more as a down lineman to fill in. And that's not my game. So I had one and a half sacks in that whole stretch. Not as if I wasn't doing my job—I was bringing the pressure, harassing QBs, forcing guys to throw high, which is when interceptions happen. And the arrangement was working—we were winning. It just wasn't as much fun. And when I'm not having fun, I'm not firing up the team. It began to show. We had lost to the Bills, and we went into a two-game mini-slump, dropping games to the Eagles and the Niners.

The next week we played the Vikings, who were trying to keep their playoff chances alive. They were desperate. They played desperate. They

came out running reverses, tight-end screens, bootlegs, all kinds of garbage. Herschel Walker was mowing us down like he was cutting the lawn. The worst part was they were setting the tempo, dictating the game to us. That wasn't Giants football.

When we went into the locker room at halftime we were losing, 12-10. Their offense had taken it to us for 175 yards. I figured it was time for the team captain to step up.

I told the guys they weren't being physical enough. I told them we had to gang-tackle those mothers. "I'm going to start playing the way we're supposed to play," I said. "If anybody wants to come along, fine."

Hey, I'm no Martin Luther King. I'm not even a Harry Carson. Most of the time when I got up and said something I had no idea what I was going to say, and afterward I would have no idea what it was I'd said. Basically, my leadership style was to play my game. If guys wanted to follow, they knew what to do.

And when we hit the field in the second half, we stopped getting our butt kicked and started kicking butt.

Me in particular. Carl had finally come back from his injury, and we were clicking again up front. I was one happy dog, off its leash, just running wild.

I had two and a half sacks.

I stripped the ball from Rich Gannon.

I got right in Gannon's face in another play and got him to toss the ball away—for an INT.

I made twelve tackles.

I stretched out and got Herschel Walker by the ankle to prevent a TD.

And, oh yeah, we won. Clinched the division, too.

Man, after that game we felt like we were ready to go. Bring on the playoffs! Bring on the Niners! They had won four Super Bowls, including the last two in a row—everybody knew the road to Tampa went through San Francisco.

But there were three more games left to the regular season. The next one was against Buffalo. Jim Kelly was the top-rated quarterback in the league, and their defense was nails behind their stud end, Bruce Smith. He was saying going into the game that he was the best defensive player in the league. We'd see about that.

It ended up being an ugly game. Icy, wet, cold, nobody in the stands 'cause they couldn't drive to the stadium. Hard to grab the frigging ball, too. Our center, Bart Oates, sailed one way into the backfield. I couldn't get my hands on two sure interceptions. And the ugliest part, aside from us losing the game, was that we lost Phil Simms for the year. He sprained his foot on a sack, tried to play on it, but just screwed it up worse. We got ours when we got Kelly in the knee and knocked him out of the game. Like I say, ugly.

We ended up losing, 17-13. Jeff Hostetler replaced Simms when he went down. I wasn't sure about this guy...he sure as hell wasn't a Phil Simms. Didn't look like someone who could take us to the promised land.

But in the final games against Phoenix and New England, Hoss proved me wrong. He was sharp in his passing, but the thing with him was that he had a motor. Not to take anything away from Phil, but Hostetler's legs gave us something we didn't have at QB before. He could give us yards on the ground—83 against the Patriots—but also give the receivers time to create separation just by running around until something opened up.

We finished out the regular season 13-3. We were going to the playoffs again, and there were no ifs, ands, buts, doubts or any other crap getting in our way. We weren't taking any prisoners against Chicago in the first round.

We buried them, 31-3.

Hoss was nails again, throwing for TDs, running for TDs. Belichick was brillant, too. He put us in a 4-3 defense—ofttimes a 6-1, with Carl Banks and me on either end of the line. The aim was to mess with Mike Ditka's complex run-blocking schemes to neutralize Neal Anderson, their new Walter Payton. We'd closed our practices all week to work on that damn thing. Almost like another training camp. Pain in the butt, especially for guys like me who'd been in a 3-4 for the last decade. But it worked. The Bears got 27 yards rushing. Total.

One down. One to go: San Francisco. No surprise there.

Fine with us. We knew we were going to have to strap it on for this one, but we had a lot of unfinished business with Frisco. Just that year we'd lost a frustrating one to them. And too many times since I'd started with the Giants the 49ers had been the ones keeping us out of the Super Bowl.

I got to take back a little of what I said before about the Niners. Yeah, they were dirty cut-blockers, but they were also one of those teams that made you take your game to the next level. The Redskins were another one of those teams you looked forward to playing. Washington generally played our type of football. Physical, straight-ahead ball where you knew you were gonna have to play your best, with John Riggins coming at you like a freight train every single down.

The 49ers tested you in a different way. Their "West Coast Offense" had more finesse, style and complex schemes. They were also at their peak, with Joe Montana, Jerry Rice, Ronnie Lott, guys who would eat you

for breakfast if you let 'em. They'd won four Super Bowls in the last nine years, had just won two in a row and were going for a three-peat. The two games we played against them that year—this playoff game and an earlier game that we lost 7-3, were two of the most memorable games I'd played the whole time I was in the NFL.

Just about every athlete will tell you about "the zone." Those times when you are playing beyond yourself, totally plugged into the moment, when everything outside the game is blocked out. The NFC Championship game was like that. It was just our eleven people and their eleven people—nothing else existed. We fought hard throughout the game. I had no sense of time—no idea of how much time was left on the clock, no idea of what quarter we were in or what the score was. Just a battle that went on and on and on in the best way, everybody on both sides of the ball playing 100 percent...man, I'm telling you, I got totally lost in the game.

My stats in that game were not much to look at. One tackle, half a sack. But numbers don't tell the whole story. At this stage in my career, offensive coordinators were keying their whole game plan around me. So right there I'm screwing with them before the game's started. Giving my teammates chances, too. But here, like in a lot of other games, there were "big play" moves I made that didn't show up in the game summary. Here's one:

Late in the fourth quarter the Niners had the lead, and the ball. Montana was marching the team downfield. It was 13-9. They wanted to put it out of reach.

Montana called a play that was rolling to our right. Everybody went with it. But then Montana, who had those quick feet, spins and rolls out the other way. I'm shadowing the guy from the middle—I switch directions

PAGE
190

same time as he does and rush over the left side to cut him off. Joe has a man downfield—sees me coming—tucks it in—cuts away to my right just as I go by with my claw out—spots his man—pumps again and—WHAM. Leonard Marshall rams his helmet into Montana's back. Joe crumples. The football squirts out. We recover.

Leonard laid it out on that play. One of the greatest I had ever seen him make—or anyone else, come to that. He'd come in from Joe's blind side and been blocked into the ground by Bubba Paris, their big-ass tackle. He dragged himself up toward Montana, fell down again, got up again and launched himself at Joe.

It was a clean play, too—and it was absolutely nails. Montana's season was over.

But what bought Leonard the time to crawl his way into that sack was me hunting Montana down from the other side.

Now we had the ball, but we had to make it count. Three downs and we weren't getting anywhere, though. Damn. Punt. Except my boy Gary Reasons, the blocking back on the punt team, spotted a hole in their line big enough to drive a Mack truck through. He called for the snap short and Mack-trucked it 30 yards downfield. As usual, the Giants D was leading the way. A couple plays later we had another field goal. We were still one point down, though. With the time running out. We had to get another turnover. And the Niners knew it. They weren't taking chances. They were running it. Roger Craig kept moving the chains with that high-stepping, dick-busting stride. Now they were at our 30 with 2:42 left. Steve Young gave to Craig. Craig burst over left guard. Our noseguard, Erik Howard, was being double-teamed by their center and guard—and pushed out of the play. But Howard's not only big and yoked, he's a *sneaky* dog. He went down on one knee, like *Oh, darn, I'm out of this one.* The center, Jesse Sapolu, bought it, started looking around for someone else to take out. Erik immediately hauled himself up and dove between Sapolu and the guard, Guy McIntyre—right into Craig's stomach. The ball flew out of Craig's hands—and yours truly was there to catch it.

We ran a few plays as the clock ran out. Matt Bahr was rock solid that day. With no time left—all these big studs standing on the Giants sideline holding hands to will it through the crossbars—he kicked his fifth field goal with no time left to send us to Super Bowl XXV.

I ran up and hugged Matt. Nearly squeezed the life out of him.

That, right there, is what I played for. My game was more than just violence and intensity and adrenaline. When the game is at its best, there's just something that takes you outside yourself. It's the one thing that really scratched that itch, the thing that really fulfilled me.

Sometimes…sometimes I thought about what I was gonna do when I didn't have the game anymore. But there was no thinking about that now.

The New York Giants were on their way to Tampa!

We were pumped. Well, who isn't pumped for a Super Bowl? I was calling random Tampa numbers from my cell phone and telling people the Giants were coming to kick booty!

Our United flight attendants were all wearing NEW YORK GIANTS—1990 NFC CHAMPIONS T-shirts, and Pepper Johnson was our in-flight deejay. One conga line started, and then another. We're talking twenty-plus 250-300-pound. guys dancing up and down the aisle of the plane. I'm surprised the goddamn thing didn't flip over.

The pregame buildup was one big hype job. Bill told us he was going to be hyping the Bills big time, talking about how great they were, Jim Kelly this, Bruce Smith that, wow, we're just here to play our best. "Don't believe a word of it," he said. "I'm going to blow Buffalo one big smokescreen all week. Let 'em start believing how good they are."

Seemed like it was working. Bill saw a picture of some of them in a jewelry store getting sized for their Super Bowl rings. I tried some little psych jobs of my own. I went to a Tampa club with Erik Howard, Steve DeOssie and Jumbo Elliot, the OT who'd be lined up across from Bruce Smith on game day. Then, what do you know, Bruce Smith, Jim Kelly and

some of the other big Bills sit down near us. Bruce had a bit of an ego—blazer, no shirt and a big gold "BRUCE" hanging from a chain around his neck. I decided to play with his head a little bit. "You dirty dogs!" I jumped up out of my chair, screaming at them. "Jumbo's gonna kick your tail, Bruce!"

Jumbo was embarrassed—well, maybe scared. But he was up for that game, and got more than his share of butt-kicking in against Bruce.

We had been pretty sure we could handle the Broncos in Super Bowl XXI. The Bills, though, were a hell of a team. Kelly was one of the top quarterbacks in the NFL, no doubt. Thurman Thomas could bang out yards, Andre Reed and James Lofton were dangerous receivers and their defense was on par with ours. And just five weeks before, they'd beaten us. Taken out our top gun, too. Hoss had been playing in Phil's place way better than anyone expected. But hey, now, the Super Bowl was still only his fifth start.

Usually, the Giants way is to play straight-ahead, smashmouth football, and to play it a lot harder and better than you. Here, it might not be enough just to kick the bejeezus out of 'em. We needed an edge.

We looked to our own Bills, Parcells and Belichick. They did not disappoint.

The thing about the Buffalo Bills' offense was that it was so quick. They had this hurry-up, no-huddle approach that had caused headaches around the league. Lots of teams have used it since, but the Bills were one of the first. And Jim Kelly was a master at running it.

So we had to jam them up, chew up as much of the clock as we could.

Parcells designed an offense that was going to eat minutes: lots of running, keeping it inbounds the whole time. "Power wins football games," he said. Ottis Anderson executed perfectly. He got 102 yards, but most important, he helped us keep the ball for over 40 minutes. MVP material, for sure.

On defense, Belichick mixed it up big time. In December, the Bills had Reed coming over the middle for a busload of yards and Lofton zapping us for long gains—not to mention Thomas running up our butt. Belichick wanted to contain Buffalo's total attack. So we did the exact opposite of the 5-2 we'd gone with to stop Chicago's run game. He had two down linemen, with me rotating in as a third rusher on some plays. He put in our safety, Dave Duerson, at linebacker to shadow Thurman Thomas. Give Thomas some room to run a bit—not too much, but enough to keep Kelly from fixing his mind on the pass. Meanwhile, Belichick crowded the backfield with DBs in nickel-and-dime sets to neutralize Lofton. Everson Walls made the defensive calls from a deep safety position.

I didn't particularly like the setup. Containment's not my game. And I didn't get to play as much. But when it shut those guys down in the second half, I had to admit it was genius.

There was more in Belichick's bag of tricks, though.

You look at those tapes. We're kicking the ball away from where the officials spotted it—*aw, woops!* We're creating pileups the size of Mount Rushmore, guys jumping on five minutes after the tackle has been made. And we're coming off of those piles like blue sludge. He told us—like he wanted this to happen, almost—that if we got hurt, not to move. "Don't limp off the field," he said. "Let the trainer come out to you." Anything to slow…the game…dowwnnn. It worked, too. Instead of throwing our timing off, we were the ones messing with the Bills' rhythm.

Belichick. Dude's an *evil* genius.

'Cause every second we ate up counted. It was that tough a game, and that close.

With 2:16 left in the fourth quarter, our lead just 19-17, Kelly got the ball back on his own 10-yard line. He and the Bills were fast enough to march that bad boy upfield all the way to our 29. Kelly spiked the ball with eight seconds on the clock. Their field goal team came on. This was it. The whole game, the whole season, the whole enchilada. *No way* I was coming out of the game. If we were going down, I had to know that I was there, doing what I could. I stayed in and lined up next to Erik Howard.

I had a vision of leaping up and blocking Scott Norwood's kick in *the* most spectacular Super Bowl finish of all time—and the perfect ending to the LT highlight reel. They counted out the snap, a lot of heavy mothers crashed together—and I got a mouthful of turf instead. I didn't even want to watch it go through the uprights.

Turns out it never did.

I heard the noise, and later I saw a tape of Norwood's kick sailing...wide...right! Awwwwwww, yeah!

World Champions!

Sloosh! Bill Parcells got an instant Gatorade shower. I grabbed Carl Banks, my co-captain. "Let's go, baby," I told him. "We got to give the coach a ride!" We were on top of the world.

In all the noise, the hollering, the lights, the confetti, I didn't think about what Bill Parcells had told me the week before the game. It was a good thing I didn't. Instead of a victory celebration, it might have felt more like a funeral procession or something.

'Cause that was really the beginning of the end of my football career.

CHAPTER 10 | The Will To Hit

Going Out Standing Up

Super Bowl XXV was the last game I ever played for Bill Parcells. He'd told me a couple weeks before that he was leaving the Giants.

He left for a lot of reasons. There were power issues between him and George Young, and his relationship with Wellington Mara and the new co-owner, Bob Tisch, was not real good. He'd also made some noise about wanting to build a franchise somewhere else as general manager *and* coach. And maybe he saw that, even though we'd just won a Super Bowl, the team was probably going to be going downhill from there.

In the end it was probably just time for him to move on.

But it still hit me hard. Bill and I had talked about going out together. I'd even thought if he went to another team I'd go there. But he was going into the broadcasting booth as an NBC analyst.

I'd never played on an NFL team without Bill. I wasn't sure I wanted to play for anyone else. Or even could. I can be, you might say, a difficult guy. Motivation-wise, I need special handling. Bill was maybe the one guy in the world cut out for the job. In the ten years I played under him, there had been plenty of bad times when I'd just thought about throwing it in. But Bill was able to keep me going every time. Encouraging, dissing, baiting, challenging—whatever it took, he got me out there, bringing it.

In retrospect, I probably should have just carried Bill out of Tampa Stadium, kept going and not looked back. It wasn't my greatest game, but it might have been the last time I played with fire in my gut.

Bill leaving was just the biggest chunk in a whole landslide coming down that year.

In the best of times—well, in the Bill Parcells era—the Giants didn't seem to be able to handle winning. Me, I had no problem with being #1— a season without a championship was like a day without sunshine. But after '81, when we were suddenly good and had made the playoffs for the first time since '63, and after our first Super Bowl, the team had gone into the crapper. Guys lost focus, egos were out of control. Team first became me first.

Some of the guys couldn't handle the pressure of being champions. Win a Super Bowl, wear a target on your chest the next year. All of that was happening big time in '91, and as usual, losing made it worse.

What made it worse yet was Ray Handley, who'd taken over as coach. Dude could not handle a team. Where Bill was a heartburn special with all the fixin's, Handley was vanilla. He was so focused on not offending anyone that he didn't please *anyone*. Not the press, not the 8,000,000

critics outside Giants Stadium and not his players. Guys didn't sense authority from him. They didn't give him respect.

Guys were teeing off directly on Handley in meetings. There was one time I even had to pull Carl Banks off of him when Carl had him pinned up against a wall. It was no surprise when we went from the Super Bowl to an 8-8 season in '91, and 6-10 in '92.

Now the Giants defense had always taken pride in itself. And even in the worst of times, when the defense was dragging, the linebacking unit was nails. But that was in the Parcells/Belichick years. And Belichick was gone, too. After he nailed Buffalo's offense in the Super Bowl, the secret was out: the whole league realized the guy was a genius. He got a good offer to go to Cleveland as head coach, and he went with it. Yeah, some of the guys clashed with Belichick's anal, detail-obsessed style—me, for instance—but Rod Rust, the new defensive coordinator, was making those the good old days. Handley brought in Rod Rust, and Rust brought in the "Read and React" defense.

The Read and React was supposed to be a good complement to a 3-4 defense. And maybe in some other universe it was. But it wasn't Giants defense. You can't dictate a game when you're reading and reacting. Come on now—you might as well be sitting in front of a television! A *true* Giants defense *made the offense react to us.*

So right away, I started jamming up that scheme. On the field, I had my boy Steve DeOssie calling Belichick's schemes instead of Rust's. Hung Steve out to dry when Rust called him on it, too!

It was not a happy time for anyone on the Big Blue Wrecking Crew. Particularly for me. With Bill gone, all the roller-coaster fatigue, all the baggage I'd collected in ten years of playing in the NFL my way, all of it was suddenly dumping down on me. I'd always looked forward to the start of the season. After a sweaty training camp, working my way back into shape, I wanted to get out there and get high from good, hard, helmet-banging contact. But as the 1991 season started to fart away like an untied balloon, something was definitely missing.

I just did not feel the will to hit.

For me, that was the sign that it was over. Or that it would be real soon.

Because in good times and bad I had always had that one thing: hitting. Contact. Getting the man's head to snap back, feeling him jerk as you axed him and sent an electric shock through his body, watching him crumple down to the turf, the ball bouncing free, the crowd roaring. Like I said, I felt like that's why I'd been put here. I was a warrior. I'm no student of history, but any kid knows every culture all throughout time had its warriors. The guys that strapped on the armor or even just picked up a spear, went out to defend their women, kill buffalo, take a dude's scalp—hey, that was me! And to do that, you had to have rage.

Ronnie Lott talked about that in a book he wrote. He said that the fierce competitors have got rage bursting out all over the place. Mike Singletary splitting his helmets all the time. Me, ripping the bottom of my cleats off when I'd blast off on ballcarriers. It wasn't that I was actually angry at these guys—I really respected most of the players in the NFL—but come game time, man, I wanted to kill those dogs! I wanted to take heads off, tear arms off, rip their guts out. That's *rage*.

Ronnie Lott knows about rage. This is a dude who mangled his finger in Timmy Newsome's face mask and had a doctor cut half of it off just so he could keep playing. Ronnie's a warrior—one of the greatest players football ever had.

"Not to be disrespectful to Carl Banks and the other Giant linebackers," he wrote, "but their rage isn't anywhere near that of LT's. Even if one of them slipped on a #56 jersey, the difference in emotion would be very obvious."

Here's what else he said: *"LT wears his rage like a shield."*

Oh, yeah.

Now, well, maybe I was ticked off at Rod Rust and frustrated with Ray Handley, but I didn't feel rage. Maybe rage is a young man's emotion. All I really felt was sad. And tired. I realized Bill could have worked those ingredients into some first-class rage. But Bill was gone…and I was 34 years old. My rage wasn't there. And without it, I didn't have my shield.

No warrior wants to go out there without his shield.

When Handley took over, he had a talk with me. He told me how much he wanted me on his team, painting this great picture of how things were going to be. "We have an opportunity to keep something special going," he said. Well, yeah. I guess I got suckered into going after the opportunity. But we wasted it.

Oh, I went in there and did my thing, all right. Remember, this is a guy who could come in straight from a night out, no sleep, and still go out there and get four sacks.

November 1, 1992, we're going up against the Washington Redskins. Ray Handley's a marked man. At the Meadowlands the week before, fans were singing "Ray must go!" to the tune of the Atlanta Braves' Tomahawk Chop. At 4-4 we're either holding on to a wild-card hope—or on our way down the tubes.

Rod Rust has finally canned the Read and React and is letting the Giants D play like the Giants D. Maybe it's just a reflex, but I'm starting to get into it a little bit more, maybe starting to work up a little of that old fire.

It's early in the fourth quarter. The Skins are at midfield and they're driving. They've put Don Warren, the tight end, on me all game. He's done a good job…for a tight end. I'm still in Rypien's face for way too many plays. That's one of the reasons we're leading, 24-7.

Now it's time to bring the hammer.

At the snap I fly around the outside of Warren and turn the corner. Rypien's setting up to pass when I slam into him from his blind side. The air goes out of my lungs as I absorb the hit, my eyes close, my jaw slams shut, my teeth rattle, the shock wave goes through my body like a bomb. But I keep going, driving straight through the hit, bringing my right arm down onto his, *wham,* and then—*strrrrrip!* The ball bounces away from him. We recover.

Awww, yeah. I could still bring it. Maybe not as often, but *mmm,* I could still bring the business!

A few plays later, we kick a field goal to put the game on ice.

Not a bad way to go out, I thought. Get a few more of those bad boys, give 'em something to remember me by. Take the team to the playoffs again, that'd be something, and then retire. I'd decided 1992 was going to be it. I would leave at the end of the season.

Count on fate to put a twist into my plans, though.

The very next week, against the Green Bay Packers, I was having another LT game. Since we'd beaten the Redskins the week before and actually had a winning record, every game, every series of downs counted if we were gonna get a playoff spot.

Now, I was a "big play" guy. Coaches said I had a nose for the hinge play, made the stuff happen when it counted. "Big plays" are mostly BS, ofttimes just crowd-pleasers. Like a meaningless sack that people go wild for—even though the other team makes a touchdown pass on the very next play. But I knew the game well enough to recognize the three or four plays that really mattered in a game.

You can just feel it in the air. It might be when you're up by 14 points, but you know if the other team scores on that play, it's back in the game. It could be a play at the end of the game, or a chance to put a team away for keeps early. There are guys who shun those moments. Like in basketball, some guys will pass off on the pressure situations. But Michael Jordan wants to take that last shot—he will *demand* it. He doesn't want Scottie Pippen or anyone else taking it.

I want to take that shot, too. You put the whole game on the line, the whole season—that's my moment. I was going to find a way to make the play. As I was getting older it might mean conserving my energy until that moment came, but I was going to make it.

In the first quarter I grabbed Brett Favre for a six-yard loss, then batted away a pass. I took a low leap at their running back, Vince Workman, wrapped him up around his midsection and got the strip. We recovered and got a TD out of it. I came out with a shoulder injury, had them give it some wrapping and came back in.

Late in the third quarter, we're holding onto a 13-7 lead. Favre is marching the Packers again. Time to go into the phone booth and put on the Superman cape. Favre throws, I leap—I get a hand on it! Yes! *Two* passes batted down! *Not bad for an old man*, I think as I land on my stomach. But then I realize nobody's got the ball yet—it's still live!

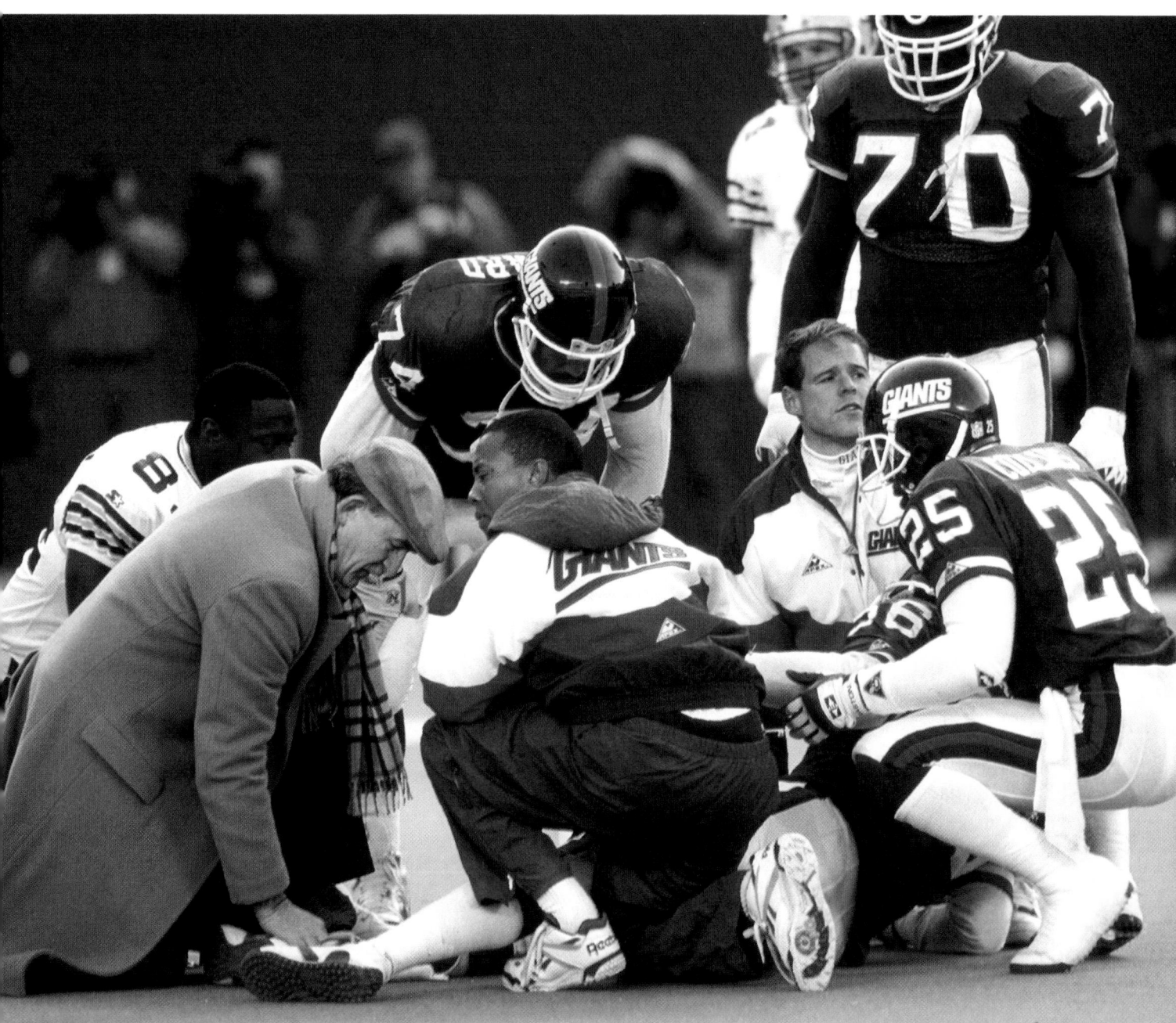

I get myself up to spot it and grab it, but somebody shoves me down and I feel a *snap* and *oh, MAN*, it's like somebody's shot me right through the ankle. I'm lying there, screaming, my whole ankle in flames. They bring the cart out. I get myself together a little bit and tell everybody I'm gonna walk off under my own power. A warrior leaves the field standing up, or else he doesn't leave it at all.

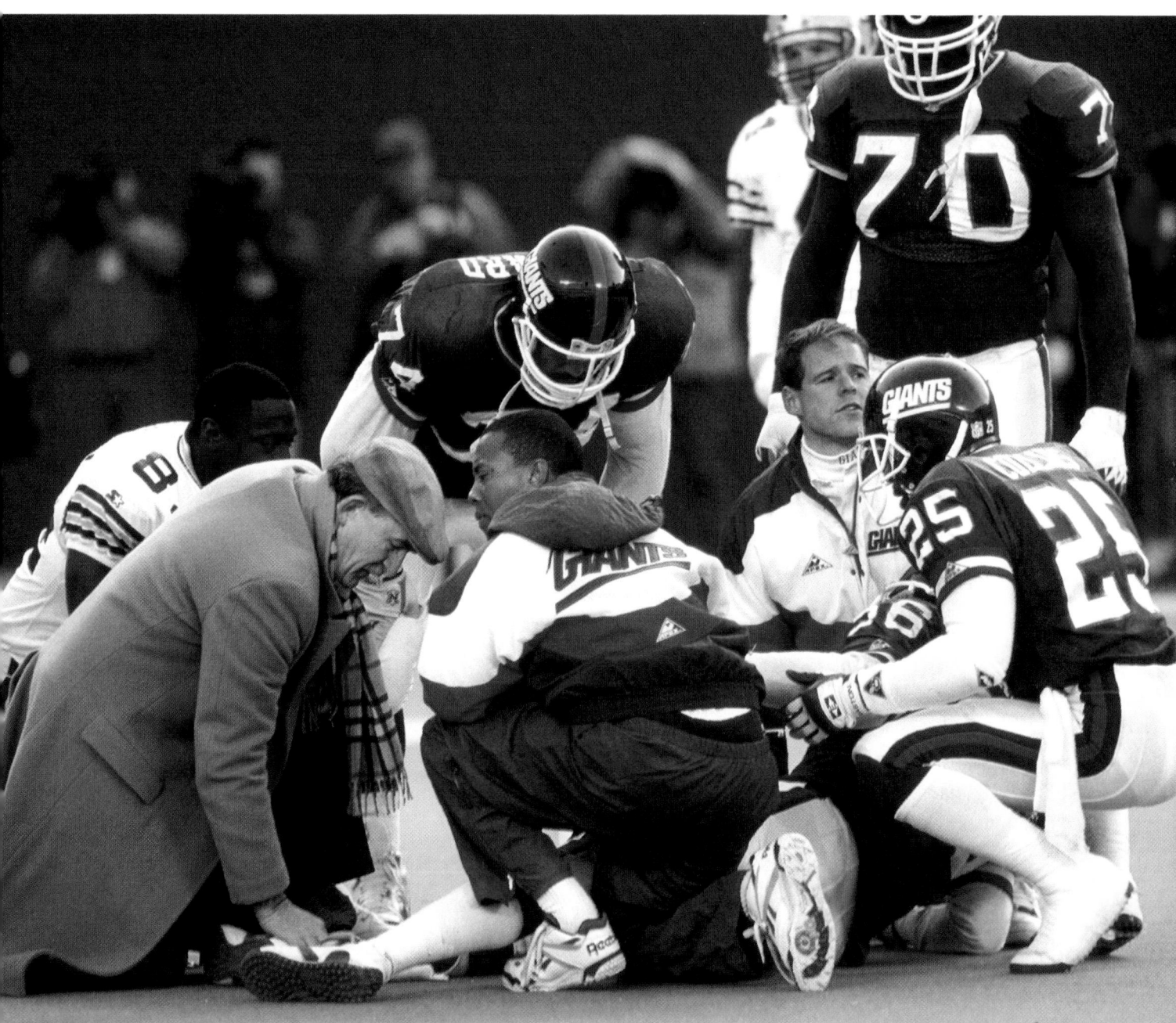

"I wanted to go out on my feet, at full speed...

ideally knocking the snot out of some quarterback."

But *ahhhhh*, I can't even frigging stand up. No strength in that ankle—and way too much pain. Carl Banks and Erik Howard lift me and put me on the cart. So much for my big play.

I went in for Achilles tendon surgery the next day. The surgery went well. My recovery was so fast that, as usual, everybody was amazed. I even went on record as saying I'd be ready by January for the playoffs. Fortunately for me, I guess, we never got close. The Giants ended up losing six out of the next seven games. Ray Handley was the obvious scapegoat. He got the axe, along with Rod Rust.

So as I recovered, I spent some time thinking. It was such a bad way for it to end, being wheeled off on a damn golf cart. I wanted to go out on my feet, at full speed, ideally knocking the snot out of some quarterback. I wanted to go out like a man, in other words, not a frigging invalid. Even though I said I'd be gone at the end of the '92 season, like everything else, I wanted it to be on *my* terms.

In March, I told George Young that I was coming back.

By this time, the Giants had signed Dan Reeves as head coach. He made it clear right away that he was going to be running a tight ship. He blew a fuse because I didn't attend minicamp. Minicamp? Come on, Dan. I think I attended minicamp once the whole time I was a Giant: my rookie year. I dropped in from a golf tournament to talk to him about it. We came to an understanding.

Dan Reeves was a good football man. He'd gotten the Broncos to the Super Bowl and felt like eventually he could get us there, too. He didn't pussyfoot around doing it, either. Like Parcells, he cut guys who were friends of mine because he felt the team needed fresh blood. Right from the start it was clear the Handley era was over. No more dissing the coach to his face, no more mutinies. Dan got the guys' respect, got them having fun again. Mainly, he got them winning. And Mike Nolan was a breath of fresh air as defensive coordinator. A smart guy who understood what we could do. I hope he's able to turn the Niners around and start mixin' it up in Frisco.

My last tour of duty with the Giants started in Chicago. Phil Simms and I had a throwback day, both of us old Giants. Phil passed for 277 yards. I had four tackles, two sacks and stripped Jim Harbaugh to shut down their last drive and end the game.

This 34-year-old still had game.

Yeah, there was a time when saying I was old was throwing down a challenge. When I was 29 or 30, if anybody called me old and washed-up, come Sunday I'd kick his team's teeth in. After that, I started getting a little more realistic with myself. Those suicide plays I was running in '81? Jumping over blockers? I wouldn't even think of it at 32. I was afraid someone would cut my knees. Now, at 34, everything was hurting. When I got up in the morning, it sounded like I was making popcorn. (And let me tell you, there's a lot more popcorn now.)

I'd been able to balance my physical decline with more smarts, more experience. Building on my mental database of tells, looks, schemes. Toward the end of my career, the main thing was picking my spots. Like a boxer, I had to know when to go rope-a-dope and when to get my punches in.

In reality, 1993 was a year when I was a threat more than a terror. I was still getting guys like Mark Rypien to be looking around for me at the line of scrimmage, just like old Jaworski. I was usually double-teamed, too. I was hurt, though, more hamstring business. I had six sacks and 76 tackles, but in a lot of games I wasn't a real factor.

It was time.

Except for Phil, just about all the guys I'd played with over the years were gone. I'd outlasted 'em all. Reeves had cut my friends Steve DeOssie and Pepper Johnson earlier in the year. Carl Banks, Gary Reasons, Leonard Marshall and a dozen others had been traded, cut, retired or free-agencied off the team. I felt kind of alone. The people around me were young dudes whose names I couldn't remember. Sometimes I'd just call 'em by their numbers.

It was time.

Everybody had been speculating about my retirement for the whole season. But when I decided to come back after my Achilles tendon, I'd made my mind up that whatever happened, 1993 would be my last year. I told a few friends, otherwise kept it quiet. I didn't want the whole damn year to be about LT. That was a distraction no one needed, especially now that we were playing playoff football once again.

We had homefield advantage for our wild-card game against the Vikings. It was five below. Giants weather. But when we went to the locker room at halftime, we were the ones getting frozen out. We were down 10-3 and could hear boos as we went through the tunnel. It was not much of an LT game. I had three tackles, had deflected a pass and was in their quarterbacks' faces a lot of times.

By the old LT standards, it was like I wasn't even there. I wasn't chasing the 4.4 guys—just getting a good seat and watching 'em. But I still had the LT mystique.

Even if I didn't know all our young guys' names, I could still light a fire under their rears.

Some of the older guys got up and said things in the locker room, talked about the importance of the playoffs. I got up last. I never knew what I was gonna say. I just got up and turned on the flamethrower.

"The Vikings…" I made a face. "Sheeoot, these @#$%!&ing punks shouldn't even be on the same *field* as us!"

That got their attention.

"We got to put them *away* in the second half!" I walked around, looking guys in the eye, shaking some people, punching shoulder pads.

"Don't just be happy to be in the playoffs, son! If you're *happy*, you gonna be sitting at *home* next week!"

I looked at them. Then I turned it up a notch and screamed, *"NO MORE SCORING!!"*

I don't know. Maybe that had an effect. All I know is that we went back out there and stomped them. Kept them away from the end zone, scored two TDs ourselves and won, 17-10.

The crowd was pumped. They were up and rocking, 75,000 people. As the clock wound down, they were cheering, *"LT! LT! LT!"*

I hadn't said anything publicly about my retirement. Still, it was just one of those things that was out there, so obvious you didn't need to have a press conference. People knew this was my last home game. It was their last chance to reach out, wrap me up, connect with me. A hundred guys in Giants hard hats hanging down over the railing with their arms stretched out as we ran back through the tunnel, *"LT! LT! LT! LT!"*

Here's what I found out: at five below, your tears freeze.

We flew out to Frisco for the divisional playoffs...and got kicked in the nuts. It was like a lot of our young guys were in awe instead of in a playoff game. They were watching Ricky Watters run on us and Steve Young fire missiles to Jerry Rice and John Taylor like it was TV. The Niner D, now, they didn't get near the props we got, but *unnh*—they were a wall. It never frigging seemed to stop until in the end they'd piled 44 points onto our 3. One of our guys said the turning point in the game was the national anthem.

Maybe at one time Superman could have changed that game around all by himself. But Superman was hanging up his cape.

I tackled Ricky Watters once, and got an assist. Maybe not the game I'd like to have gone out on.

But it was time.

I announced my retirement in the little room at Candlestick Park after the game.

"I've done everything I can do. I've been to Super Bowls. I've done things that other people haven't been able to do."

Somebody asked me what I was feeling.

What was I feeling? Here I was leaving pretty much the only life I'd known, a life where I knew who I was, where I was going and why I was getting up in the morning. (If I went to bed, that is.) And now all of that was over.

What was I feeling? There was so much going on inside my heart it was like I was numb. Like I couldn't feel anything at all.

"I'm going to miss just being around the guys," I finally said. "I've been playing with the Giants for thirteen years. It seems like I've been in the locker room thousands and thousands and thousands of times. It's been my world for a lot of years. To change that and go in a different direction…Instead of making that left turn to go down to the locker room, I'll be going up toward the stands…"

Game Over

From Hell to the Hall

August 7, 1999

Almost six years after the clock ran down on my last game, I experienced the greatest moment in my career when I was inducted into the Pro Football Hall of Fame.

There was a lot of noise going in about whether with my life outside of football I should be elected to the Hall. But until you stand up there and look down at that bust, and then look out at your comrades, your coaches, your fans, you can't understand how much bigger the Hall is than any of that. As my son T. J. said that day, it's the place where legends live. I wish I had the words to tell you what an honor it is to be there...but I don't.

I can tell you that my induction was a time to mend some fences, to heal some wounds, to resolve and reconcile.

The first thing, which really knocked me out, was my son T.J.'s introduction. For a kid who didn't have the easiest go of it with his dad, I was floored by the way he stepped up and said he wanted to do it—and by what he had to say. T.J. said people admired LT the football player, "but I admire Lawrence Taylor, my father." We hugged for a long time after that, right there on stage. I said some private things to him. I also damn near broke down and cried like a baby. But I was able not to. Didn't think it would be, you know, appropriate.

When I stepped up to the mike, I thanked about a zillion people. I thanked my family, and Linda, and my kids big time. I thanked my teammates. I singled out Harry Carson, who really showed what a big man he was by showing up that day, honoring me and setting aside any differences we had. I thanked Bill Parcells, George Young and Wellington Mara for taking a chance on me. And for standing by me. Which in my case sometimes took a lot of balls.

And oh yeah—something else I couldn't forget looking out at all the blue Giants hardhats in the audience. I thanked the fans, those crazy, wonderful mothers.

"LT! LT! LT! LT! LT!"

So what does it mean, being enshrined in the Hall of Fame?

What does it mean to have been one of the wildest men in a wild game? To have lived life at full speed, balls out, no compromises, no apologies? To never have done anything halfway?

What does it all mean? I've thought a lot about that. And I think I said it best in the way I wrapped up my speech:

"You know, people ask me all the time, well, you're in the Hall of Fame. What do you want to leave to other people? What do you want other people to remember? What kind of legacy do you want to leave behind? And I thought about that...the thing I want to leave all the people is that, you guys, life, like anything else, can knock you down. It can turn you out. You'll have problems every day in your life. But sometimes... sometimes you just got to go play. You just got to go play. And no matter how many times it knocks you down. No matter how many times you think you can't go forward. No matter how many times things just don't go right. You know, anybody can quit. Anybody can do that. A Hall of Famer never quits. A Hall of Famer realizes that, a Hall of Famer realizes that the crime is not being knocked down, the crime is not getting up again."

November 16, 1987
Veterans Stadium
Philadelphia

Reporters were asking Coach Buddy Ryan about the Philadelphia Eagles' game with us that week. Ryan said the key to the game was his 24-year-old quarterback, Randall Cunningham. Cunningham, he said, was a faster runner than Walter Payton.

"The only player that can catch Randall in the league is #56. And I'm not sure he can do it this year."

The guys put that up on our bulletin board. They wanted to see what I was going to do with it.

With the media, I was like, aw, shucks.

"He's probably right," I told the papers. "Cunningham's been running away from a lot of people. He's not the same guy we knew last year…I might not be able to catch him. If I can, I can. If I can't, I can't. We'll find out Sunday."

But here's what Buddy was really saying: *Cunningham's too fast. And at 28, LT's just a step too slow.*

And here's what LT was saying: *Buddy, no one throws down on me.*

Come game day, the Eagles were playing very physical ball, as usual, and the game was going back and forth. I got two sacks on Cunningham when he tried to scramble over the middle. Couldn't quite catch him when he angled toward the sidelines, though. I could get him out of bounds, but not bring him down. I had to say this: the dude was fast. Very fast.

In the fourth quarter, with the clock running down, it was 20-17, Giants. Cunningham and the Eagles kept driving, though, hoping to get a TD to win it, or at least a better field position to get a field goal to send it into overtime.

Sorry, son. Can't give you that.

With the players' strike that had started the season, we had to win this game and all the others if we were gonna have any chance of making the playoffs. We had to shut them down—now.

It was 3rd and 4. The Eagles are on our 26-yard line. Only 33 seconds on the clock. The look they're giving us says *pass*. But with Cunningham there's always a good chance something else is gonna happen.

At the snap, Cunningham rolls out to his right, like he's looking for a man downfield. I've been shadowing him, working my way across the center. Jim Burt, Leonard Marshall and the other guys are battling out in the trench in front of me. Got to pick the right line here. Whole game's turning on the angle I take. If I go straight in to hit him while he's passing, I'll miss if he runs. Second-guess him to the outside for the run—he throws to Quick or Toney and we could lose right there.

Bottom line: he can't get that first down. He gets first down, they get four more downs. They get four more downs, they win the game. They win the game, no playoffs.

He can't get that first down.

And there's no one that can keep him from getting it but me.

I keep drifting, drifting…but I'm smelling run. I just know Cunningham's faking the pass…what he's doing is clearing out a running lane for himself…and then he goes. Brings down the ball and sprints full bore toward the sideline. I'm with him, running when he runs, a missile straight at him and NOW I put every last bit of juice I've got into my legs and launch myself through the air at him. The air goes out of my lungs, I feel the hit down to my toes as I crash into that bad boy just as he's about to turn upfield—we're a yard short of the first down marker. I'm wrapping him up, making sure he doesn't move forward another *inch*, and I'm taking him down. I'm rolling over with him when *AAAGHH*, it feels like someone's jabbed a hot poker below my butt! What the…?! I stay down, grabbing my leg. Cunningham gets up, looks at the down marker…walks off the field. Fourth down.

The Eagles' field goal team comes on. I'm still on the ground. Finally two of our trainers come over from our sideline, lift me up and help me off the field. The poker still feels like it's buried in my thigh—it's the hamstring. I wonder if I can even play next week. I've *got* to play!

But like everyone else, I'm watching them set up for the kick with eleven seconds left. Paul McFadden, their kicker, lines up. He walks backwards, no shoe on his kicking foot. He paces off to his left. Some of the guys are saying he's usually good from this distance.

The snap. The place. The kick…for the tie…is…wide…*left!*

Pandemonium on the Giants sideline. You'd think we just won the damn Super Bowl instead of getting ourselves to 3-6.

With some help, I limp through the tunnel and into the training room. I hear dudes hooting and hollering from the locker room. The trainers put me up on the table and start working on me, taking a look at the hamstring, poking around.

I'm lying down, wincing. It feels like knives.

Bill Parcells walks in and just stands there, looking at me, shaking his head. I see him out of the corner of my eye.

"Hey, Coach!"

"Yeah, Lawrence?"

I raise my head up and look over at him.

"Tell Buddy that I can still catch 'em."

Lawrence Taylor's Sacks, Quarterback-By-Quarterback

Quarterback	Sacks
Randall Cunningham	12.5
Ron Jaworski	12.5
Neil Lomax	12.0
Joe Theismann	8.0
Jay Schroeder	8.0
Steve DeBerg	7.0
Gary Hogeboom	7.0
Danny White	5.0
Rusty Hilger	5.0
Lynn Dickey	4.5
Troy Aikman	4.0
Mark Rypien	4.0
Bob Gagliano	3.5
Steve Pelluer	3.0
Bernie Kosar	3.0
Bobby Hebert	3.0
Tommy Kramer	2.5
Rich Gannon	2.5
Richard Todd	2.0
Steve Grogan	2.0
Brian Mcclure	2.0
Steve Beurlein	2.0
Tom Tupa	2.0
Marc Wilson	2.0
Jim Harbaugh	1.5
Jim Kelly	1.5
David Whitehurst	1.0
Pat Haden	1.0
Steve Bartkowski	1.0
Gary Danielson	1.0
Archie Manning	1.0
Boomer Esiason	1.0
Dave Wilson	1.0
Scott Brunner	1.0
Randy Wright	1.0
Frank Reich	1.0
Timm Rosenbach	1.0
Jim Everett	1.0
Vinny Testaverde	1.0
Steve Young	1.0
Stan Gelbaugh	1.0
Brett Favre	1.0
Wade Wilson	1.0
Jim Zorn	0.5
Dan Fouts	0.5
Bill Kenney	0.5
Warren Moon	0.5
Dan Marino	0.5
Andre Ware	0.5
Total Sacks	**142.0**

Tackles, Regular Season
Solo Tackles 828
Assited Tackles 260
Total **1088**

Tackles, Post Season
Solo Tackles 50
Assited Tackles 24
Total **74**

Tackles, Career Total
Solo Tackles 878
Assited Tackles 284
Total **1162**

Year	Sacks
1981	9.5
1982	7.5
1983	9.0
1984	11.5
1985	13.0
1986	20.5
1987	12.0
1988	15.5
1989	15.0
1990	10.5
1991	7.0
1992	5.0
1993	6.0
Career Total	**142.0**

Awards

1986
AP Defensive Player of the Year
AP NFL MVP
Bert Bell MVP Trophy (Maxwell Club)
PFWA MVP
UPI NFC Defensive Player of the Year

1983
UPI NFC Defensive Player of the Year

1982
AP Defensive Player of the Year

1981
AP Defensive Player of the Year
AP Defensive Rookie of the Year

Acknowledgments

Thanks to Douglas Gorney for an outstanding writing job, Jerry Pinkus for providing the perfect photographs, and my agent Mark Lepselter for his guidance and advice throughout this entire project.

To my parents who have always stood beside me, my kids who I thank God for every day, and all the men and women, girls and boys who cheered for me when I played.

56

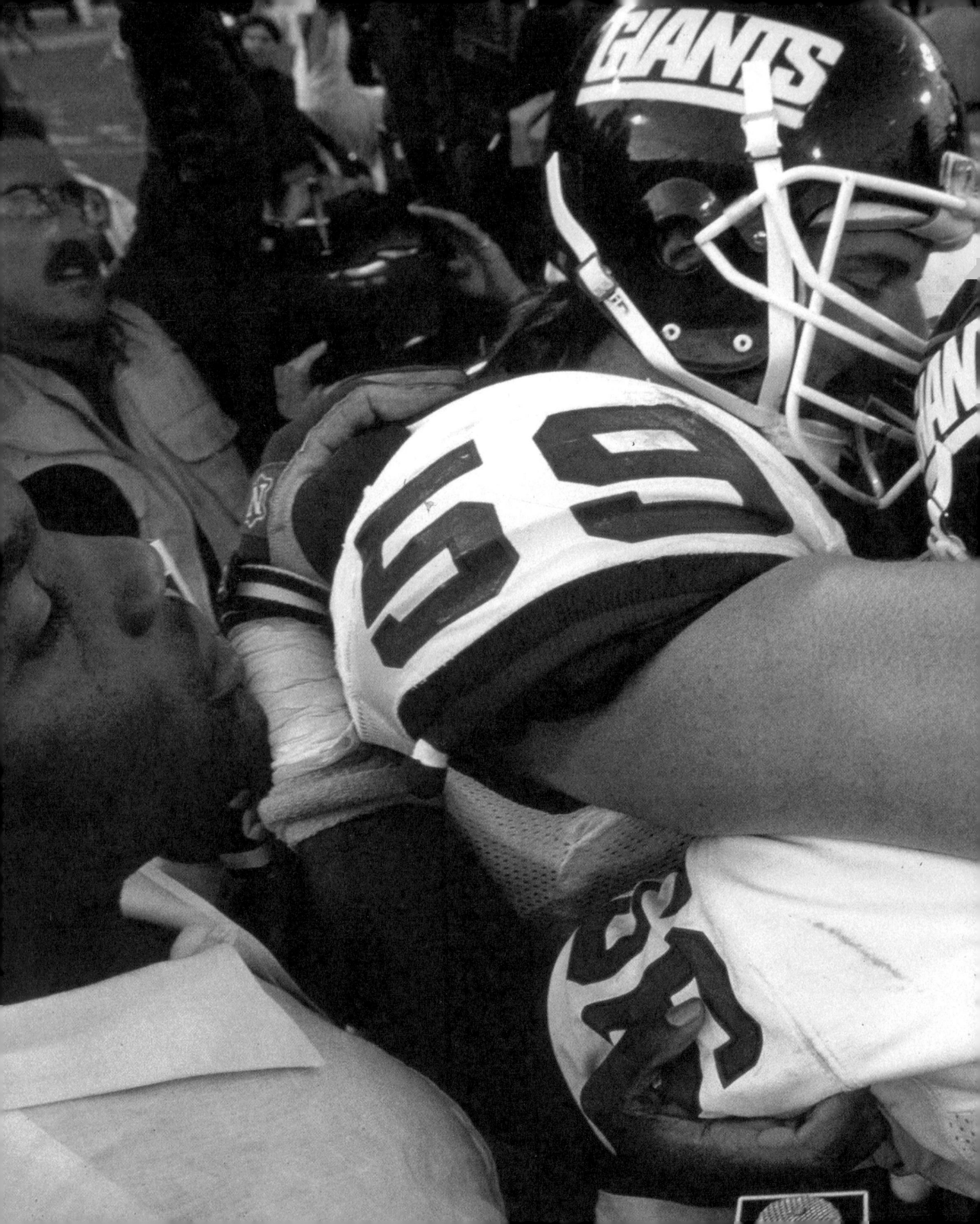